MAKING DOLLS and DOLLS' CLOTHES

MAKING DOLLS *and* DOLLS' CLOTHES

76 complete patterns for dolls and dolls' outfits

Lia van Steenderen

Translated by Mary Berclouw—Baden.

First published in the United Kingdom in 1988 by
Exley Publications Ltd,
16 Chalk Hill, Watford, Herts WD1 4BN.

British Library Cataloguing in Publication Data

Steenderen, Lia van
    Making dolls clothes.
    1. Doll clothes
    I. Title   II. Poppen & Kleertjes. *English*
      745.592′2   TT175.7

      ISBN 1-85015-098-2

Originally published by Elmar Publications
© Lia van Steenderen

Drawings and cover: Lia van Steenderen

Printed and bound in Hungary

Contents

Foreword

A book full of home-made dolls' clothes and clothes for children up to the age of seven.

The smallest doll is a cuddly little thing measuring 4" (10cm): it can easily be fitted into a coat pocket and taken to nursery school. It consists simply of a head and a body. The larger rag dolls have arms and legs and they are equipped with clothes which can be put on and taken off.

Then there is a set of clothes for baby dolls 11½" (29cm), 14" (36cm) and 17" (43cm) long, which you can buy. You will find everything that the baby doll needs, from sleeping sack to underwear, pants and jackets. From tiny mittens, scarf and hat for chilly days to airy clothes for boiling hot weather. The portable crib is very handy to take out; naturally the doll will then be wearing her special outdoor clothes!

Dolls who are past the baby stage, standing-up dolls, are, of course, more demanding as far as clothes are concerned. They won't wear just anything any more, they like to follow fashion. That is why in addition to the practical things that you just have to have, like jackets, dresses, pants and night clothes, they also have a jogging suit, a bodywarmer and legwarmers and there is a real Japanese kimono. Lots of clothes, like overalls, can be worn by boy and girl dolls.

The fathers and mothers of the dolls are also taken into account. If they are not older than seven, they can wear the same clothes as the dolls. The patterns for their clothes are in the book, together with the patterns for the dolls' clothes and the rag dolls. The sewing instructions are set out clearly next to the patterns.

Introduction

Materials

The children's clothes and dolls' clothes in this book can be made out of almost any material. It is best to choose easily washable fabrics that don't run. If you don't like the shade of a piece of cloth, you can dye it first. Textile dyes can be bought at supermarkets and department stores. Cotton can easily be washed at quite high temperatures. This is very handy for children's or dolls' clothes, which can become very soiled. Cotton material may shrink the first time it is washed. It is therefore advisable to wash new cotton material before cutting it out to fit the pattern. Wool needs very careful washing. Wash only by hand and never in too hot or too cold water. If very frequently washed, wool may become matted or felted.

Some types of materials

BATISTE:	Fine light cotton or linen fabric like cambric.
BOUCLE:	Material knitted or woven from specially looped yarn which gives a curly look.
CORDUROY:	Coarse or fine ribbed cotton velvet.
CREPE:	The yarn is exceedingly twisted during weaving. It is crease-resistant.
DENIM:	Strong cotton material.
FLANNEL:	Soft woollen fabric of open texture with a light nap.
FLANNELETTE:	Brushed cotton fabric.
GABARDINE:	Smooth durable twill woven cloth.
GLAZED COTTON:	A cotton fabric covered with a layer of lacquer.
HONEYCOMB/THERMAL:	Fabric woven with a pattern of raised hexagons or squares.
JACQUARD:	Figured woven material made of cotton, linen or half-linen. Damask patterns stand out from the ground fabric with a contrasting sheen.
TICKING:	Tough linen or cotton material, usually striped.
TERRYCLOTH:	Soft, absorbent cotton fabric consisting of many tiny loops.
STRETCH TERRYCLOTH:	The same but of a finer consistency and stretchable.
VIYELLA:	Fine, soft quality half-woollen flannel.

Different materials can make very good combinations. Some examples are:
Glazed cotton lined with brushed flannel or corduroy.
Corduroy combined with shiny cotton (pockets, casing etc.)
Shiny cotton combined with terrycloth.
Honeycomb/thermal combined with flannelette.

Quilted material

It is quite easy to make your own quilted material. The outer layer and the inner layer can be made of cotton, the filling can be polyester wadding or lightweight interlining.

You can stitch straight or diagonal lines for your quilting design. You can also follow the lines of a fabric motif or applique. For transferring an applique design to fabric see the heading: applique. First baste the three pieces of cloth together and then quilt them.

You can quilt the three layers of fabric as one whole length of material first and then put the pattern on to the material and cut according to the instructions. Or, you can cut out the pattern separately from the three fabrics and quilt each pattern piece. In tnis case, add a very generous seam allowance of 2″ (5cm) because the material will be drawn together when it is quilted.

Amount of material

The amount of material has been generously calculated for the largest size. For a smaller size you can usually count on a lesser quantity, it depends on the style. For pants you can use quite a lot less material for a smaller size.

The amount of material needed for dolls' clothes has not been stated, because usually you can make a great deal out of a very small piece of material.

Taking measurements

Measure over underwear. The pattern should always be slightly bigger than the measured sizes.
1. Chest width measured over the fullest part of the chest.
2. Waist width measured around the waist.
3. Hip width measured across the fullest part of the buttocks.
4. Back length, from the base of the neck to the waist.
5. Sleeve length, from the shoulder to the wrist.
6. Skirt length, from the waist to any desired length.
7. Length of pants, from the waist to any desired length. (see diagram)

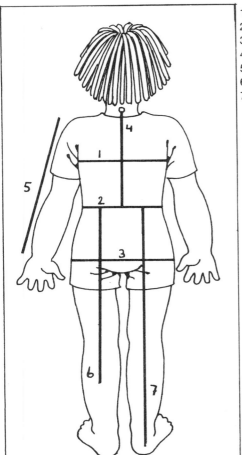

1. Chest width
2. Waist width
3. Hip width
4. Back length
5. Sleeve length
6. Skirt length
7. Length of pants

Sizes for babies and small children

If in doubt, always follow the size measurement rather than the age of your child. Size is by height of the child.

size 24" (62cm) is for about 0-3 months
size 27" (68cm) is for about 3-6 months
size 29" (74cm) is for about 6-9 months
size 31" (80cm) is for about 9 months to 1 year
size 34" (86cm) is for about 1½ years
size 36" (92cm) is for about 2 years
size 38" (98cm) is for about 3 years
size 40" (104cm) is for about 4 years
size 43" (110cm) is for about 5 years
size 45" (116cm) is for about 6 years
size 47" (122cm) is for about 7 years

Sizes for baby doll:

Length of the doll:	17"(43cm)	14"(36cm)	11½"(29cm)
Chest width:	11"(28cm)	9"(23cm)	7"(18cm)
Waist width:	11½"(29cm)	9¾"(25cm)	8¼"(21cm)
Hip width:	13½"(34cm)	11½"(29.5cm)	9¼"(24cm)
Sleeve length:	5"(13cm)	4"(10cm)	2¾"(7cm)
Upper arm width:	5"(13cm)	4¼"(11cm)	3½"(9cm)
Hand width:	4¼"(11cm)	3¾"(9.5cm)	3"(8cm)
Outside leg length:	8½"(22cm)	6¾"(17cm)	4½"(12cm)
Inside leg length:	4½"(12cm)	3¼"(8.5cm)	2"(5cm)
Thigh width:	7½"(19cm)	6¼"(16cm)	5"(13cm)
Knee width:	6½"(17cm)	5½"(14cm)	4¼"(11cm)
Foot width:	7¾"(20cm)	6½"(16.5cm)	4¾"(12cm)
Neck width:	7"(17.5cm)	6"(15cm)	4¾"(12cm)

Sizes for standing-up doll:

Length of the doll:	19½"(50cm)	15¾"(40cm)	11¾"(30cm)
Chest width:	11"(28cm)	9¼"(24cm)	8"(20cm)
Waist width:	9¾"(25cm)	8¼"(21cm)	6½"(17cm)
Hip width:	13½"(34cm)	11"(28cm)	8½"(22cm)
Sleeve length:	5½"(14cm)	4¼"(11cm)	3"(8cm)
Upper arm width:	4½"(12cm)	4"(10cm)	3"(8cm)
Hand width:	4½"(12cm)	4"(10cm)	3"(8cm)
Outside leg length:	9¼"(24cm)	7½"(19cm)	5½"(14cm)
Inside leg length:	6¾"(17cm)	5"(13cm)	3½"(9cm)
Thigh width:	7"(18cm)	6"(15cm)	4½"(12cm)
Knee width:	6¼"(16cm)	5"(13cm)	4"(10cm)
Foot width:	6¾"(17cm)	5½"(14cm)	4¼"(11cm)
Neck width:	6¾"(17cm)	6"(15cm)	4¾"(12cm)

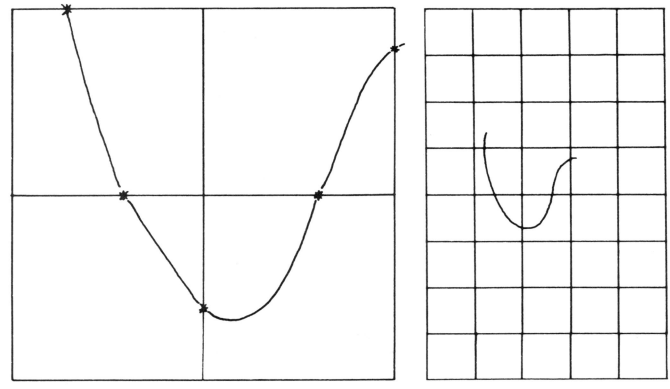

2 x 2″ (5 x 5cm)

Instructions:

The patterns are drawn to scale. If they are drawn on squares, the patterns can be reproduced on squared dressmaker's pattern paper 2 x 2″ (5 x 5cm) squares. You can buy this paper where you buy your fabric or you can draw 2 x 2″ (5 x 5cm) squares on a large sheet of paper.

The small squares vary in size throughout the book. Whatever the size, each one represents 2 x 2″ (5 x 5cm).

Mark the pattern at the points where items such as pockets, casings, loops and buttons need to be sewn on.

Reproduce the front and the back section. The section with the low neckline is always the front.

On the pattern pages, the different sizes are indicated by different lines, e.g. dotted line, solid line.

Reproducing a pattern on squared paper

Reproducing a pattern on 2 x 2″ (5 x 5cm) dressmaker's pattern paper may seem difficult to those of you who have never done it before. However, once you get started you will see that it is quite easy.

This is what to do.

Draw the longest straight line from the pattern diagram in the book on to your 2 x 2″ (5 x 5cm) squared paper. This will give you an idea of the relative proportions. From here on, mark a dot on each square of your dressmaker's pattern paper at the point where it is crossed by a line on the pattern diagram.

Having done this, you join up the dots. Watch the diagram carefully to see if the lines are straight, diagonal or curved. Don't be afraid of slight variations, it doesn't have to be absolutely accurate. (see diagram)

Sewing instructions

Always read the sewing instructions through to the end before you pin the pattern to the material and cut it out. After that, follow the instructions step by step. Read each step thoroughly before you continue sewing.

Sleeves

Sleeves that are cut out in one piece with the main garment can also be cut out and sewn on separately. Just cut the sleeves off the pattern, remembering to add a seam allowance to both pieces. For example, it is fun to make sleeves out of a different fabric. The joining seam can be disguised with a contrasting band. A row of different bands looks very cheerful (see illustration).

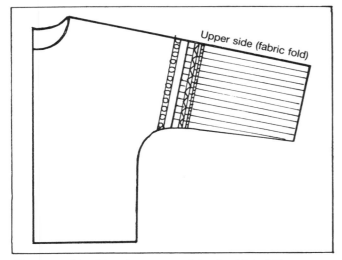

The upper side of the sleeve now adjoins the fabric fold.

Ruched lingerie elastic

When using ruched lingerie elastic in a waistline, take a length of elastic that is 2″ (5cm) less than the waist width. Stretch the elastic as you stitch the fabric, thereby giving the ruched effect.

For dolls, the waist, the leg or the wrist are measured with slightly stretched elastic. Take care that both legs, the foot or the hand can still fit through the opening. Take approx. ⅜″ -¾″ (1-2cm) extra because the elastic is to be stitched in with the side seams. For the waistline, the elastic is often cut into two pieces. One piece is sewn into the front panel and the second piece is sewn into the back panel. Then the side seams are stitched together.

Pinning and basting

Pin or baste a garment together first if there is any doubt about the fit. Follow the sewing instructions except that where stitching is indicated, you pin or baste.

Stretch fabrics

Stretch fabrics should always be sewn with a synthetic thread using a gentle zig-zag stitch so that the seams can stretch with the rest of the material.

Curved seams

Clip the seam allowance of an inner curved seam. Cut V-shaped notches in the seam allowance of an outer curved seam (see diagram).

Finishing and flattening a seam

Lay the material flat and stitch ¼″ (0.5cm) away from the seam (see illustration).

Cuffs

Knitted cuffs to add to the bottom of sleeves or the lower edge of a jacket can be bought ready-made, but you can also knit them yourself.

The cuffs should be slightly stretched while being stitched on, in order to give a puffed effect to the garment.

Bias binding

You can buy bias binding, but you can also cut the binding out of the same material as your garment or else use contrasting material. Cut the strip from the fabric on the bias – diagonally to the threads. You will often need to join several strips. Do this having the right sides together and the edges at right angles to each other. If you use the same material, you will need to buy more than indicated in the sewing instructions. Fabric that is very inclined to fray is not suitable for bias binding.

When a seam is on an inner curve, the bias binding is

stitched on more tightly. On an outer curve the bias binding is stitched on somewhat more generously. This is to prevent pulling (see diagrams 1-7).

Applique

Reproduce the design on 2 x 2″ (5 x 5cm) dressmaker's pattern paper. Now take the material on to which the design is to be transferred. Place a sheet of dressmaker's tracing paper (tracing carbon) over the position where the design is to be. Place the carbon side facing the material. Place your applique drawing on top of this.

Now trace the lines of the design with a pencil. The applique design is now transferred to the material. Now repeat the procedure to obtain different parts of the design on different pieces of material. Cut them out and iron very thin fusible webbing on to the backs (you can also use textile glue to attach appliques to garments).

Pin and baste the appliques in exactly the right positions on the design. Now attach them to the material using a zigzag stitch. Use closely-spaced, fairly large zigzag stitches. It is preferable not to use too thin or too thick fabrics for appliques. Also avoid stretch fabrics or velvet – these are difficult to work with. You could try first making an applique on a trial piece of fabric.

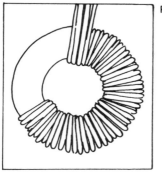
Pompom

Pompoms

You will need: two round cardboard discs of equal size with a hole in the middle. Remnants of wool or cotton yarn. With three or four strands at a time, wind the threads around the hole in the middle of the discs until it is completely filled in. (see diagram) Then cut the yarn between the two discs around the outer edge. Wind a double thread between the two discs around the cut yarn and tie it in a tight knot. Then remove the cardboard discs. Trim the pompom to make an even ball and hold it briefly over steam to make it extra fluffy.

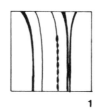 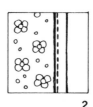 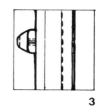

1 **2** **3**

Diagram 1
Bias binding is first stitched on to the wrong side of the material.

Diagram 2
Then fold the binding over the material and stitch it on the right side of the material.

Diagram 3
In this diagram a loop is stitched on with the binding. The loop is on top of the material.

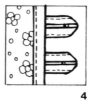  

4 **5** **6**

Diagram 4
The loop is turned to the outside and when the bias binding is folded over and stitched on the right side of the material, the loop is sewn on with it.

Diagram 5
When finishing off a collar or neckline, the end of the bias binding is first turned in. For the rest see diagrams 1 and 2.

Diagram 6
The double-stitched binding hangs out like a tie ribbon. When the binding is stitched on to the right side of the material, the length that hangs out must also be stitched twice.

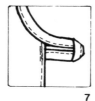

7

Diagram 7
The double stitched loose end of the binding is now folded back to form a loop, the end of which is stitched on to the back of the opening.

How to insert a zipper

Baste the opening for the zipper together along the seam line and press the edges flat. On the wrong side of the fabric, pin the zipper in position face down, with the teeth over the middle of the basted seam and the zipper tab ¼″ (0.5cm) from the top edge. Baste through all thicknesses and remove pins. On the right side, stitch the zipper in place using a zipper foot. Start at the top and stitch ¼″ (0.5cm) from the teeth, pivoting the fabric at the bottom corners. On an open-ended separating zipper, stitch down each side separately. Remove the basting thread.

Hook and eye fastening band

This is attached in two sections. One section is sewn on top of the fabric and the other underneath the fabric.
If hook and eye fastener is to be used as a middle front or middle back fastening, you should leave a section sticking out on one side (see diagram).

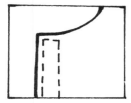

Diagram 1
Turn in the seam allowance on one side. Sew on the hook and eye fastener band. Leave a section sticking out.

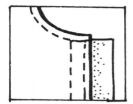

Diagram 2
Turn in the seam allowance on the other side. The hook and eye fastener band is completely sewn down on the inside.

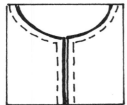

Diagram 3
The closed jacket or blouse.

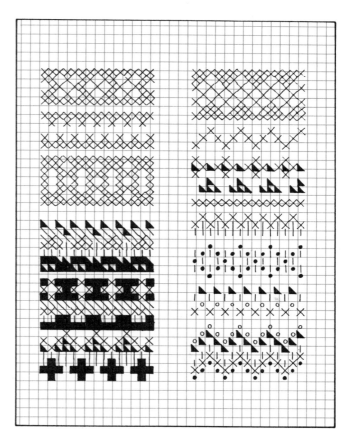

13

Knitting

Materials required:	Remnants of wool yarn, knitting needles size 9 (3.75mm).
Sampler:	11 stitches and 16 rows in tricot stitch add up to a square measuring 2¼″ x 2¼″ (6 x 6cm). 12 stitches and 14 rows in plain stitch make a square measuring 2¼″ x 2¼″ (6 x 6cm)
Stitches used:	rib stitch: 1 plain, 1 purl plain stitch: knit all the stitches plain tricot stitch: 1 row plain, 1 row purl jacquard stitch: 1 row plain, 1 row purl, knitted in different shades in different designs (see diagram)

Rag Dolls

3

4

Cuddly doll, cloth doll and miniature doll

Materials:
white unspun sheep's wool,
white, pink or beige knitted fabric,
wool or cotton knitting yarn for the hair,
soft textured cotton, cotton with a nap
or a piece of an old pullover.

Sewing instructions head and body

Head:
Take a white, beige or pink square of fabric measuring roughly 9″ (23cm). For example, a piece of an old T-shirt. Place some unspun wool or other filling in the middle of the square of fabric.

Fold in the corners to make a round ball. Add more filling until it is a tight ball measuring about 2¾″ (7cm) from top to bottom. Tie it together around the base with strong thread or cord. Cut off the loose ends of thread (diagram 1).

Sew on a strong thread at ear level. Wind the thread around the ball several times. Pull the thread tight and sew it down in the position of the second ear (diagram 2).

Now bring a thread over the top of the head, through the neck. Do not pull the thread too tight. Sew the thread down on both sides at the ear position (diagram 3).

By pulling the thread down on one side, the back of the head is formed (diagram 4).

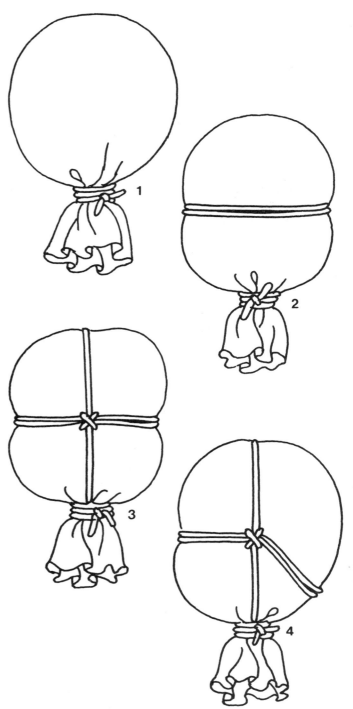

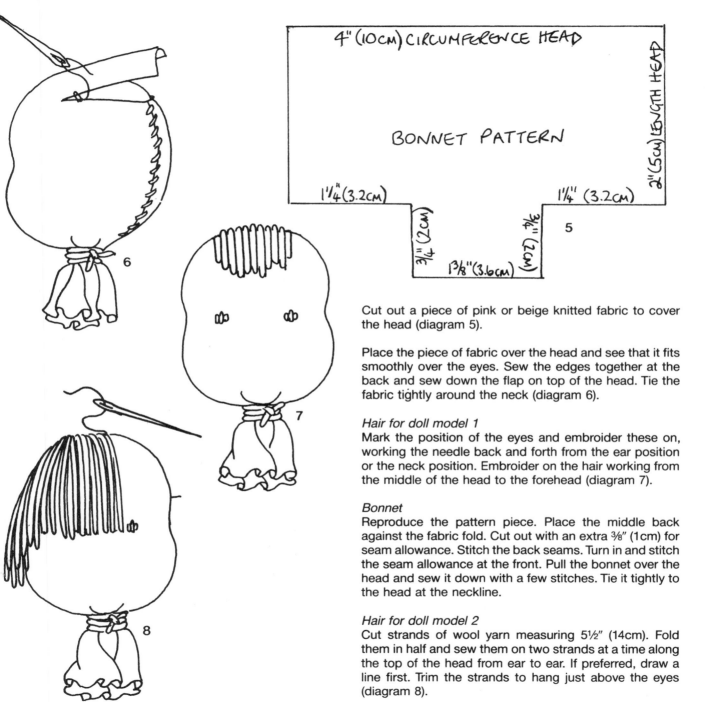

4" (10CM) CIRCUMFERENCE HEAD

2"(5CM) LENGTH HEAD

BONNET PATTERN

1¼" (3.2CM)   1¼" (3.2CM)

¾" (2CM)

¾" (2CM)

1⅜" (3.6CM)

5

6

7

8

19

Cut out a piece of pink or beige knitted fabric to cover the head (diagram 5).

Place the piece of fabric over the head and see that it fits smoothly over the eyes. Sew the edges together at the back and sew down the flap on top of the head. Tie the fabric tightly around the neck (diagram 6).

Hair for doll model 1
Mark the position of the eyes and embroider these on, working the needle back and forth from the ear position or the neck position. Embroider on the hair working from the middle of the head to the forehead (diagram 7).

Bonnet
Reproduce the pattern piece. Place the middle back against the fabric fold. Cut out with an extra ⅜" (1cm) for seam allowance. Stitch the back seams. Turn in and stitch the seam allowance at the front. Pull the bonnet over the head and sew it down with a few stitches. Tie it tightly to the head at the neckline.

Hair for doll model 2
Cut strands of wool yarn measuring 5½" (14cm). Fold them in half and sew them on two strands at a time along the top of the head from ear to ear. If preferred, draw a line first. Trim the strands to hang just above the eyes (diagram 8).

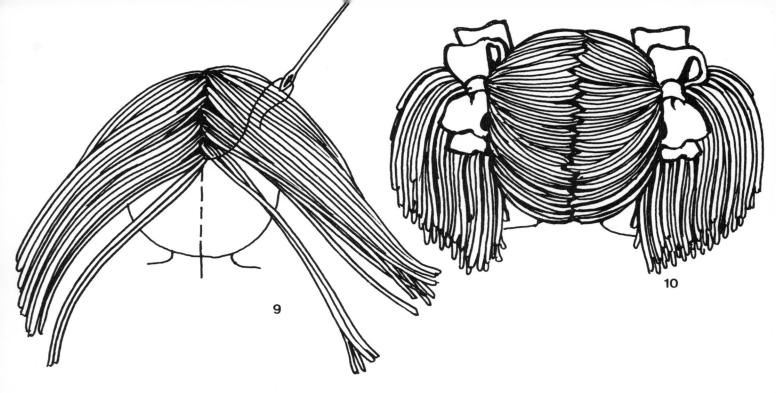

9

10

Draw a line from the front along the middle of the back of the head. Cut strands of wool yarn 11¾" (30cm) long. Sew them on two strands at a time along the middle of the back of the head (diagram 9).

Sew the bunches against the sides of the head. Tie ribbons around the bunches and trim them into shape (diagram 10).

Body
Place the pattern piece on folded fabric (knitted fabric, soft cotton or an old pullover).
Cut it out with an extra ⅜" (1cm) for seam allowance.
Stitch the body together, leaving the neck open. Clip the seam allowance all the way around and turn it right side out.
Stuff the body with filling (unspun wool, wadding, nylon scraps).
Insert the protruding flap of fabric from the neck (and the bonnet) into the neck opening. Fold in the seam allowance of the neck opening and sew this firmly to the threads encircling the neck.

Playsuit

Pattern pieces: pants front panel and pants back panel
Notions: bias binding

Sewing instructions:
1 Reproduce the pattern piece. Cut it out twice in double fabric with an extra ⅜" (1cm) for seam allowance.
2 Zigzag around the edges of the pieces.
3 Stitch the inside leg seams. Clip the curve in the seam allowance.
4 Stitch the crotch seam together all the way around. Clip the curve in the seam allowance.
5 Gather the front and the back. Finish the upper edge at the front and the back with bias binding.
6 Stitch bias binding around the armholes, leaving a length loose at the top to make a tie ribbon.
7 Stitch the side seams together.

Jacket

Pattern pieces: front panel, back panel
Notions: bias binding

Sewing instructions:

1 Reproduce the pattern pieces. Fold the fabric in half and pin the pieces to it, having the middle back against the fabric fold.
2 Cut out the neckline, the front panel and the bottom edge of the sleeves without a seam allowance. The remaining edges with an extra ⅜″ (1cm) for seam allowance.
3 Zigzag around the edges of all the pieces.
4 Stitch the upper arm seams.
5 Stitch bias binding along the edges of the front panels.
6 Stitch bias binding around the bottom edges of the sleeves.
7 Stitch bias binding around the neckline. Leave enough binding loose on both sides to tie in a bow.
8 Stitch the underarm side seams. Clip the curve in the seam allowance.
9 Turn in and stitch the hemline.
10 Make 2 pompoms and sew them on to the ends of the tie ribbons (see introduction).

Cloth doll

Take a piece of soft fabric, e.g. viyella or knitted fabric, and cut out an 18″ (45cm) square.
Stitch or embroider the edges together.
Place some unspun wool in the middle of the square and make a ball by pulling the fabric tightly around it. Push in more filling in between your fingers until the head is a taut ball about 2¼″ (6cm) high. Make sure that the head stays in the middle of your piece of fabric.
Secure the head tightly with a cord or ribbon.
Knot two corners to make hands.
Reproduce the pattern for the head scarf.

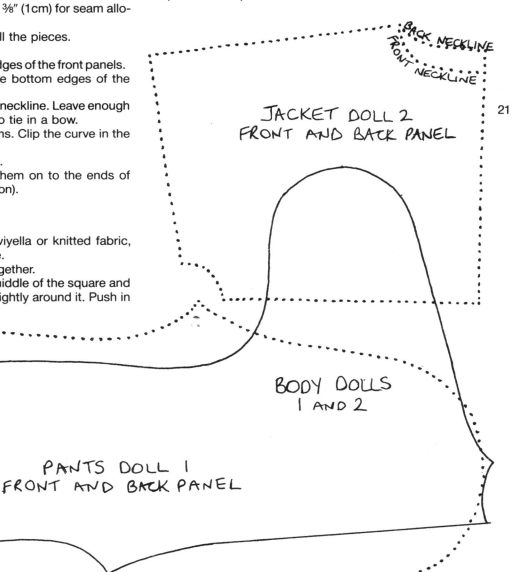

BACK NECKLINE
FRONT NECKLINE
FRONT NECKLINE

JACKET DOLL 2
FRONT AND BACK PANEL

21

BODY DOLLS
1 AND 2

PANTS DOLL 1
FRONT AND BACK PANEL

Turn in and stitch the edges and tie the scarf on to the head.
The scarf is knotted at the back of the doll's neck.
Sew the knot together and sew the scarf on to the doll's head so that the baby can't pull it off.

Miniature doll

Reproduce the pattern. Place it on folded fabric, with the middle against the fabric fold. Cut it out twice.
Stitch the pieces together all the way around but leave an opening of about 2″ (5cm) on the top. Turn the bag right side out and stuff it with filling; unspun wool, wadding or nylon scraps. Do not stuff it too tightly, it should feel nice and soft.
Make the head and the bonnet (see model 1).
Put the head into the neck opening and sew it on firmly, at the same time sewing up the whole opening.
Crochet a cord and make 2 pompoms. (See introduction.)
Sew these to the ends of the cord and tie around the neck of the doll.

22

FRONT

BONNET
DOLL 1 + 4

½ HEADSCARF

FABRIC FOLD — MIDDLE BACK BONNET

HEADSCARF DOLL 3

PATTERN DOLL 4

TOP

FABRIC FOLD

FABRIC FOLD

1

2

Cuddly doll with floppy arms and legs

Body model 1

Fold the fabric in half and pin the pattern piece to it against the fold (use knitted fabric, soft cotton or an old pullover). Cut it out twice with an extra ⅜" (1cm) for seam allowance. Stitch the body together. Leave the neck open. Clip the seam allowance all the way around and turn the right side out. Stuff the body with filling (unspun wool, wadding, nylon scraps).

Arms and body model 2

Fold the fabric in half and place the pattern against the fabric fold (use terrycloth, cotton flannel, an old pullover). Cut it out twice.
Mark the point up to which the underarm seam is to be stitched. Stitch the upper arm seam. Stitch the underarm seams together as far as the mark.
Leave the neck open.
Pull body 2 over body 1.

Head

See the sewing instructions and diagrams on page 18 (cuddly doll). In this case, the head is about 3" (8cm) high.

Finishing the head and neck

Insert the loose edges of the head (and the bonnet) into both neck openings. Turn in the seam allowance of both neck openings and sew them firmly to the threads at the base of the head.

Hands

Cut these out four times in the same material as the head.

Stitch two pieces together for each hand leaving the base of the hand open. Fill up the hands and sew them together.

Feet

Cut these out in fabric four times. Stitch two pieces together for each foot, leaving the top edge open. Clip the seam allowance of the feet. Fill them up and sew them together.

Pants

With right sides together, fold the fabric in half and pin the pattern piece to it, having the side seam against the fabric fold. Cut out the pattern piece twice.
Stitch the inside leg seams. Stitch the crotch seam together all the way around. Clip the seam allowance.
Turn in and baste the seam allowances on the ends of the legs.
Now insert the feet into the ends of the legs. Pull the basting thread tight and sew the feet on firmly.
Put some filling into the legs, not too much because the legs must remain soft.
Baste the top edge of the pants. Do *not* turn the seam allowance in while doing so. Place the base of body 1 into the pants and pull the basting thread tight. Sew the pants firmly to the body.

Finishing body 2

Turn in the seam allowance at the base of the arms and baste.
Now insert the hands into the arms. Pull the basting thread tight and sew the hands on firmly.
Put some filling into the arms, not too much because the arms must stay floppy.
Turn in the seam allowance at the base of the body. Pull the lower end of the body down over the sewn-down top of the pants and sew it on firmly.
Alternatively, sew on some tape to cover the join.

Hair

Draw a line around the head. Start from the ear position, then along the top of the forehead, along the neck and back to the ear.
Cut strands of wool yarn 16" (40cm) long. Sew them two

strands at a time along the hairline as shown in the diagram (see page 26).

Pull the hair to the back and make a ponytail. Sew the top of the tail on to the head and trim the tail to one length. Braid or plait the tail and tie a ribbon around it (see page 26).

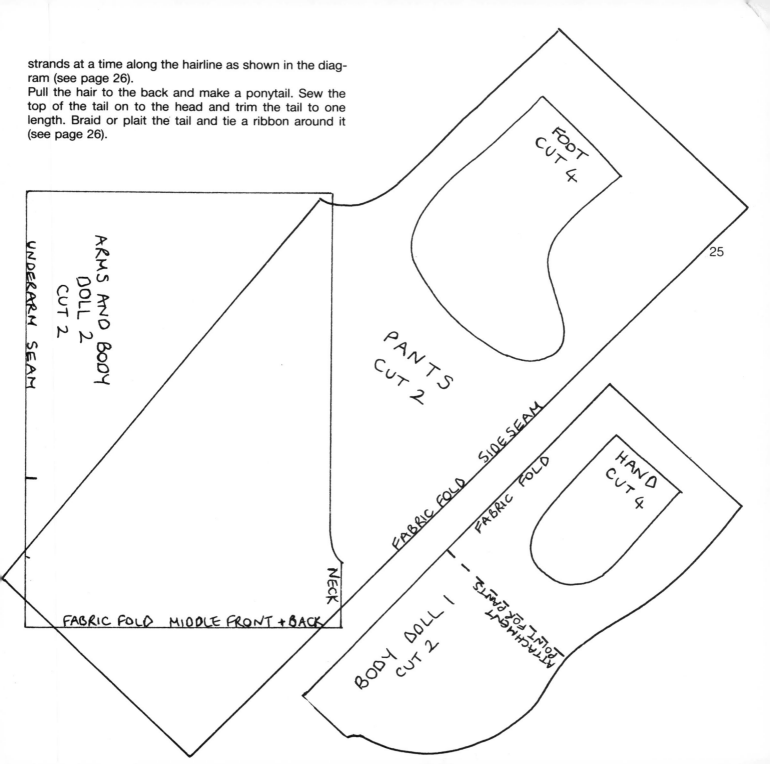

FOOT
CUT 4

25

PANTS
CUT 2

ARMS AND BODY
DOLL 2
CUT 2

UNDERARM SEAM

NECK

FABRIC FOLD   MIDDLE FRONT + BACK

FABRIC FOLD   SIDE SEAM

FABRIC FOLD

HAND
CUT 4

ATTACHMENT
POINT FOR PANTS

BODY DOLL 1
CUT 2

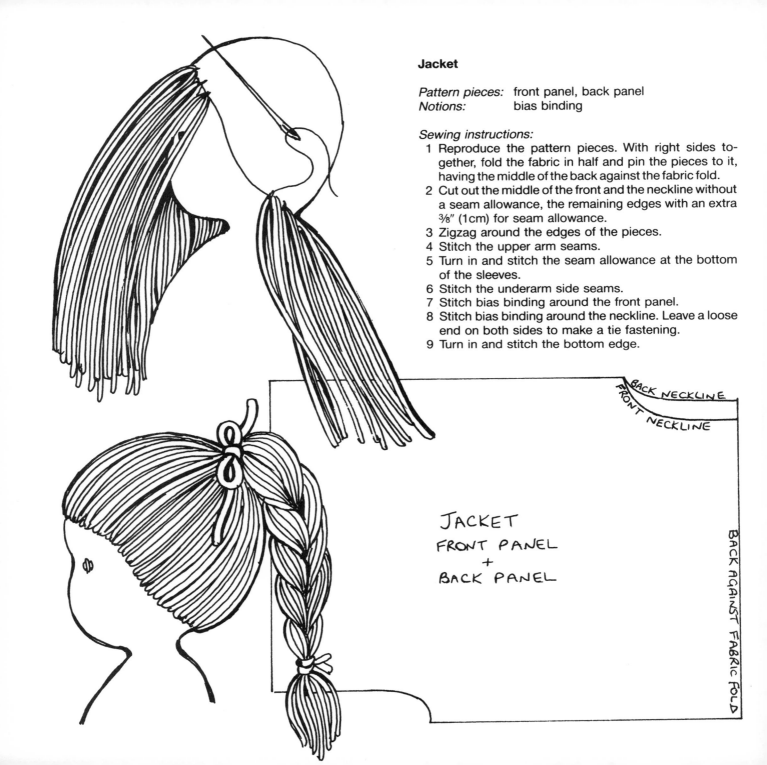

Jacket

Pattern pieces: front panel, back panel
Notions: bias binding

Sewing instructions:

1 Reproduce the pattern pieces. With right sides together, fold the fabric in half and pin the pieces to it, having the middle of the back against the fabric fold.
2 Cut out the middle of the front and the neckline without a seam allowance, the remaining edges with an extra ⅜" (1cm) for seam allowance.
3 Zigzag around the edges of the pieces.
4 Stitch the upper arm seams.
5 Turn in and stitch the seam allowance at the bottom of the sleeves.
6 Stitch the underarm side seams.
7 Stitch bias binding around the front panel.
8 Stitch bias binding around the neckline. Leave a loose end on both sides to make a tie fastening.
9 Turn in and stitch the bottom edge.

BACK NECKLINE

FRONT NECKLINE

JACKET
FRONT PANEL
+
BACK PANEL

BACK AGAINST FABRIC FOLD

4″ (10cm) Doll

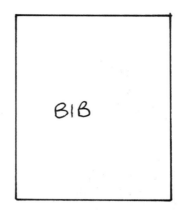

Head

For the head follow the instructions on page 18.
For this doll the head will be about 1¼″ (3cm) high. The
piece of cloth need not be bigger than a 4″ (10cm) square.
Hair: see how to make hair for the previous dolls.

Body

Use stretch fabric for the body.
With right sides together fold the fabric in half and pin
the pattern piece to it with the middle of the front and the
middle of the back against the fabric fold. Cut the piece
out twice. Stitch the body together all the way around,
leaving the neck open.
Stuff the body with filling. You could also use grains of
rice as filling.
Turn in the seam allowance of the neck. Insert the loose
edges of the head into the neck opening and sew the
body firmly to the head.

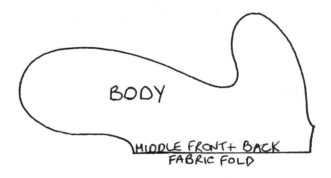

Bib

Cut out the bib in single fabric with no seam allowance.
Zigzag and then blanket stitch around the edge. Crochet
cords and sew these on to the top.

Pinafore, blouse and sleeveless jacket

With right sides together, fold the fabric in half and pin
the pattern pieces to it, having the top edge against the
fabric fold. Turn in and stitch the seam allowances of the
neckline, the sides and the lower edge. There is no seam
allowance for the sleeveless jacket – the edges are blanket
stitched and the lower part of the side seams is sewn
together.

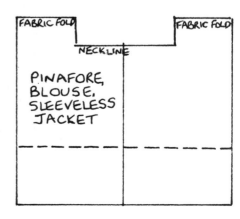

Skirt

With right sides together, fold the fabric in half and pin the pattern piece to it, with one side against the fabric fold. Turn in and stitch the seam allowance on the top edge and the bottom edge. Stitch or baste elastic around the waistline and stitch the side seam.

Neckerchief or head scarf

With right sides together, fold the fabric in half and pin the pattern to it, having the middle of the back against the fabric fold. Zigzag around the edges of the headscarf and clip the corners. Turn in and stitch the sides. Sew the headscarf on to the head with a few stitches.

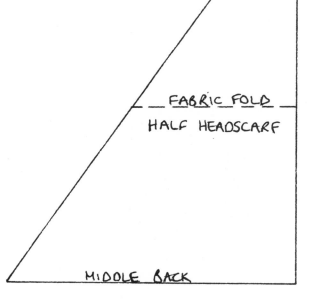

SKIRT

FABRIC FOLD

FABRIC FOLD
HALF HEADSCARF

MIDDLE BACK

BONNET

FRONT

FABRIC FOLD   MIDDLE BACK

Rag Doll

Height: 18″ (45cm) approx.
Material: 36″ (90cm) wide: 24″ (60cm) thick knitted fabric, beige or pink.
              54″ (140cm) wide: 14″ (35cm) thick knitted fabric, beige or pink.
              2oz (50g) approx. yellow, brown or beige wool yarn for the hair.
              Blue embroidery yarn for the eyes.
              Optional: red embroidery yarn for the mouth.
              Hair ribbon for doll 2.

Sewing instructions:
Reproduce the pattern pieces for the doll.
With right sides together, fold the fabric in half and pin the pieces to it. The arms and legs are cut out twice. The nose is cut out on a single layer of fabric. Cut out the pieces with an extra ⅜″ (1cm) for seam allowance.
Place the arm and leg pieces on top of each other (arm by arm and leg by leg) and stitch them together. Leave the attachment line open. Turn the pieces right side out and stuff them with filling.
Do not completely fill the very tops of the arms and legs, so that the limbs remain flexible.
Stitch the fingers where indicated.
Stitch together the middle seam on the front and the back of the head.
Stitch the front of the body to the front of the head. Stitch the back of the body to the back of the head. With the right sides together and the arms inserted where indicated, stitch these two pieces together. Leave the underneath open. Turn right side out.
Stitch the legs on to the front of the body, but leave the seam open.

Stuff the head and body firmly and sew up the underneath of the body. Gather the edge of the nose with small basting stitches. Fill the nose and pull in the gathering thread. Sew on the nose with the gathered side next to the face. By cutting out a larger or smaller circle you can make a larger or smaller nose.

The Hair

The fringe (bangs) is the same for all the dolls. Cut strands of wool yarn 8″ (20cm) long, fold them in half and sew them on, using three strands at a time, along the middle seam on top of the head. Sew in place ¾″ (2cm) away from the middle of the head and trim evenly just above the eyes (see diagram 1).

Doll 1
Cut strands of wool yarn approx 20″ (50cm) long. Sew them on along the middle of the back of the head. Draw a line from the middle back hair at the neck up to the front. Fold strands of yarn in half and sew them on along this line. Do this using 2 or 3 strands at a time, at the back and side of the head. Make two bunches of hair, sew them down and plait or braid them. Tie a ribbon on at both ends and trim them into shape (see diagrams 2, 3 and 4).

Doll 2
Follow instructions for doll 1, but start sewing on the strands 1½″ (4cm) from the middle seam on the head. Leave 4 loose strands hanging down on the forehead and trim. Sew down the bunches of hair and tie ribbons around the ends. Trim into shape (see diagrams 2, 3 and 4).

Doll 3
Using two or three strands at a time sew the wool yarn in 3 horizontal layers around the back of the head. Trim into shape around the ends (see diagram 5).

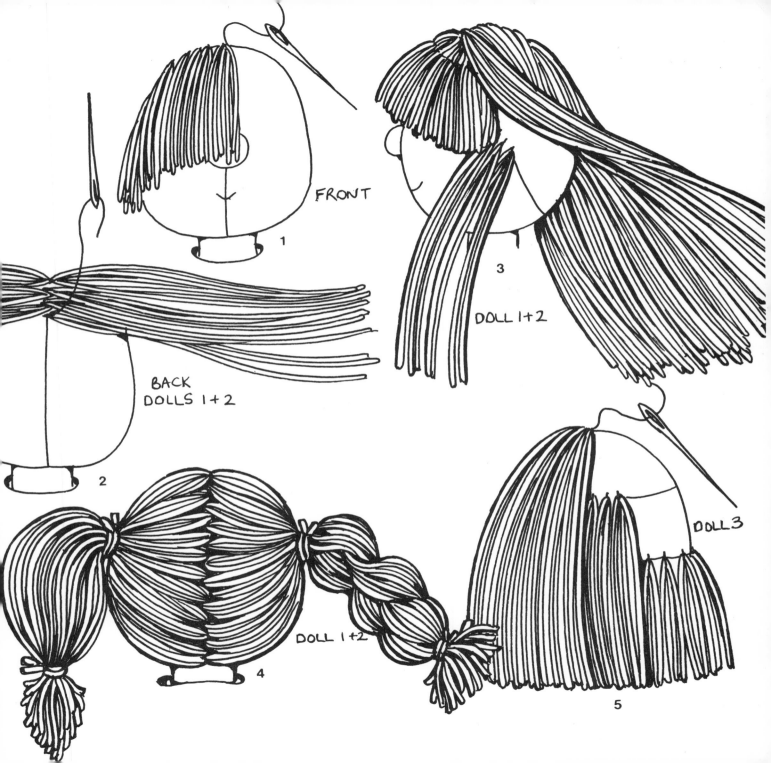

FRONT

1

BACK
DOLLS 1 + 2

2

DOLL 1+2

3

DOLL 1 +2

4

DOLL 3

5

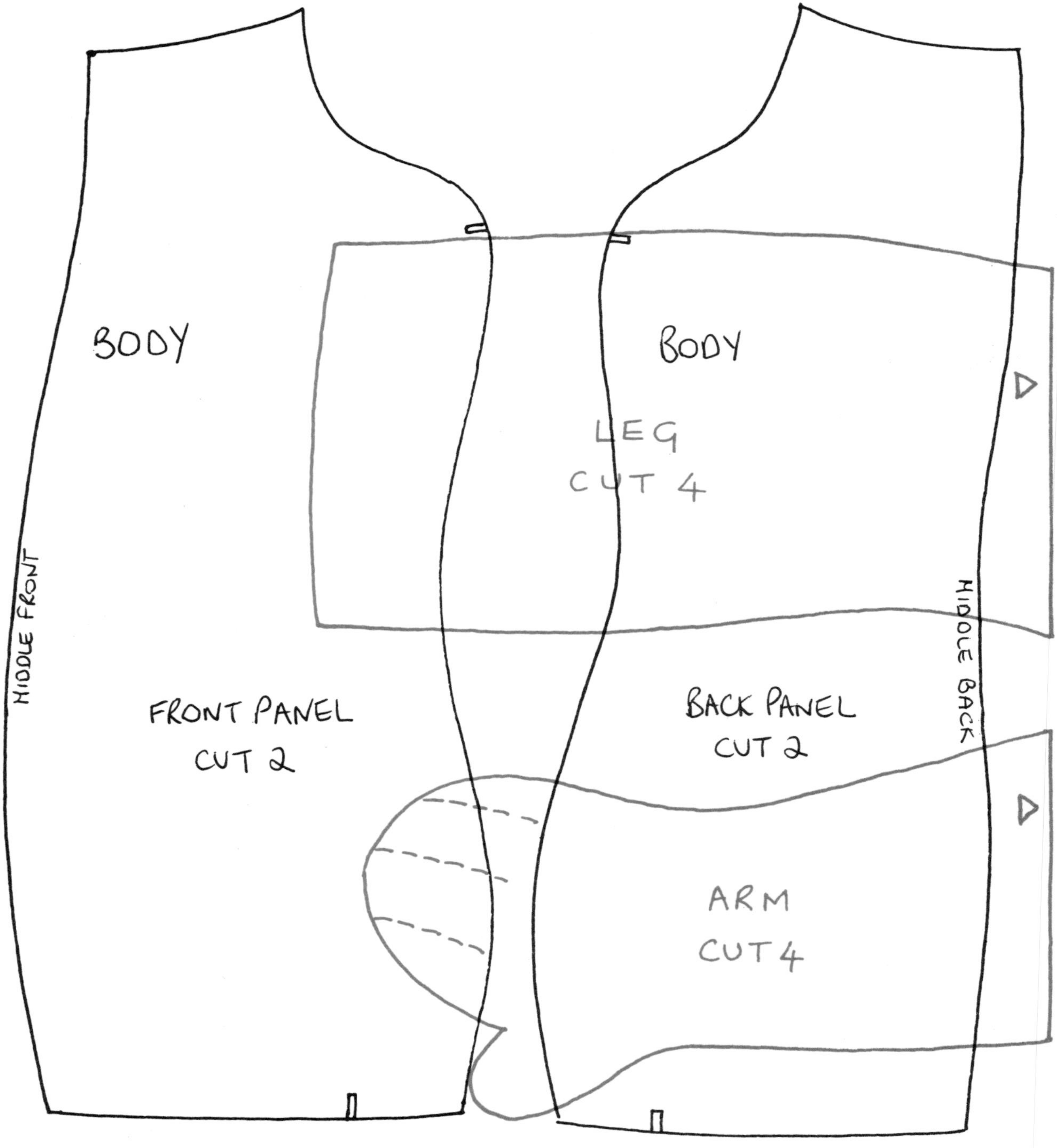

34

BODY

BODY

MIDDLE FRONT

MIDDLE BACK

LEG
CUT 4

FRONT PANEL
CUT 2

BACK PANEL
CUT 2

ARM
CUT 4

NOSE

WHEN TRACING
JOIN THE TWO
SECTIONS

WHEN TRACING
JOIN THE TWO
SECTIONS

MIDDLE FRONT

FRONT OF HEAD
CUT 2

BACK OF HEAD
CUT 2

MIDDLE BACK

Top

model 1

Pattern pieces: front panel, back panel, front neckline facing, back neckline facing.

Notions: hook and eye fastening band

Sewing instructions:

1 Reproduce the pattern pieces. With right sides together, fold the fabric in half and pin the pieces to it, having the middle of the front and the middle front facing against the fabric fold.
2 Cut out with an extra ⅜″ (1cm) for seam allowance.
3 Zigzag around the edges of all the pieces.
4 Stitch the front neckline facing to the neckline. Clip the seam allowance.
5 Stitch the back neckline facing to the back neckline. Clip the seam allowance.
6 Stitch the upper arm seams. At the same time stitch the sides of the facings. Turn in the facing and top-stitch around the neckline.
7 Turn in and stitch the bottom edges of the sleeves.
8 Stitch the underarm side seams. Clip the curves in the seam allowance.
9 Turn in and stitch the seam allowance on the hemline.
10 Turn in the seam allowance at the back and stitch pieces of hook and eye fastening band on to the back (see introduction).

Neckerchief

model 1

Sewing instructions:

1 Reproduce the pattern piece.
2 With right sides together, fold the fabric in half and pin the piece to it, having the middle against the fabric fold.
3 Zigzag around the edges of the neckerchief.
4 Cut off the corners of the seam allowance and turn in and stitch the seam allowance.

Socks

model 1

Follow the instructions for the largest size baby socks. Knit the cuffs of the socks a little longer, if preferred.

NECKERCHIEF

FABRIC FOLD

WHEN TRACING
JOIN THE TWO
SECTIONS

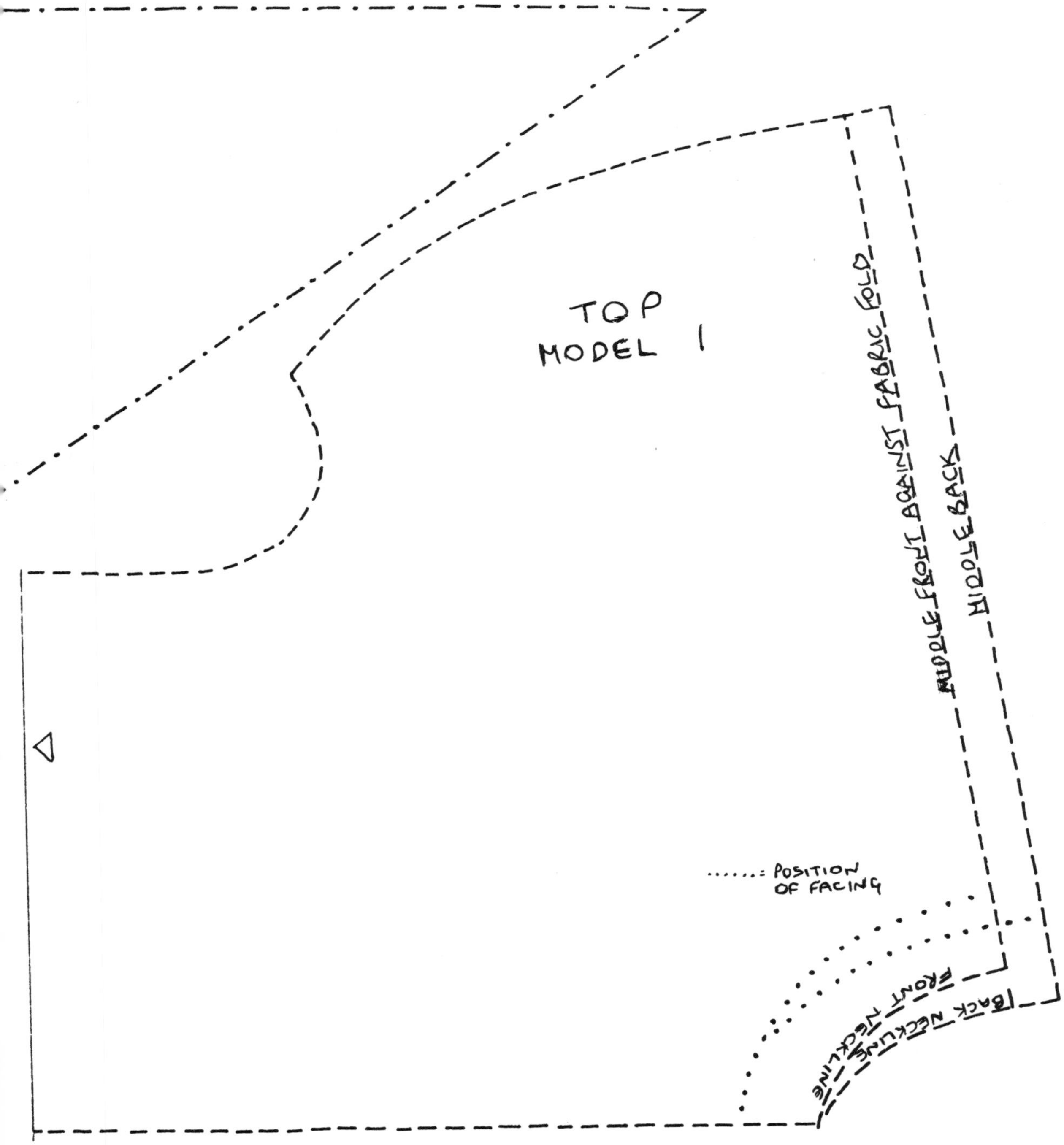

TOP
MODEL 1

37

MIDDLE FRONT AGAINST FABRIC FOLD

MIDDLE BACK

.... = POSITION
OF FACING

BACK NECKLINE

FRONT NECKLINE

Pants

Pattern pieces: pants front panel
pants back panel
Notions: ruched lingerie elastic ⅜″ (1cm) wide

model 1

Sewing instructions:
1 Reproduce the pattern pieces. With right sides together, fold the fabric in half and pin the pieces to it.
2 Cut out with an extra ⅜″ (1cm) for seam allowance.
3 Zigzag around the edges of the pieces.
4 Stitch the inside leg seams of the front and back panels together.

38

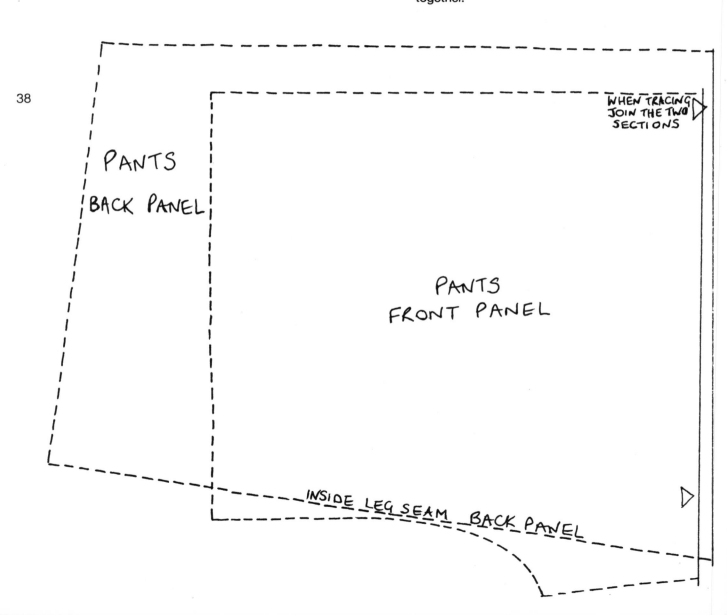

PANTS
BACK PANEL

PANTS
FRONT PANEL

WHEN TRACING
JOIN THE TWO
SECTIONS

INSIDE LEG SEAM BACK PANEL

5 Stitch the crotch seams together. Clip the curve in the seam allowance.
6 Turn in the seam allowances at the top of the pants front and the pants back. Stitch stretched ruched lingerie elastic on to the inside, so that the top of the pants are finished at the same time.

7 Turn in the seam allowance at the ends of the legs and stitch stretched ruched lingerie elastic to the inside of the ends of the legs.
8 Stitch the side seams together.

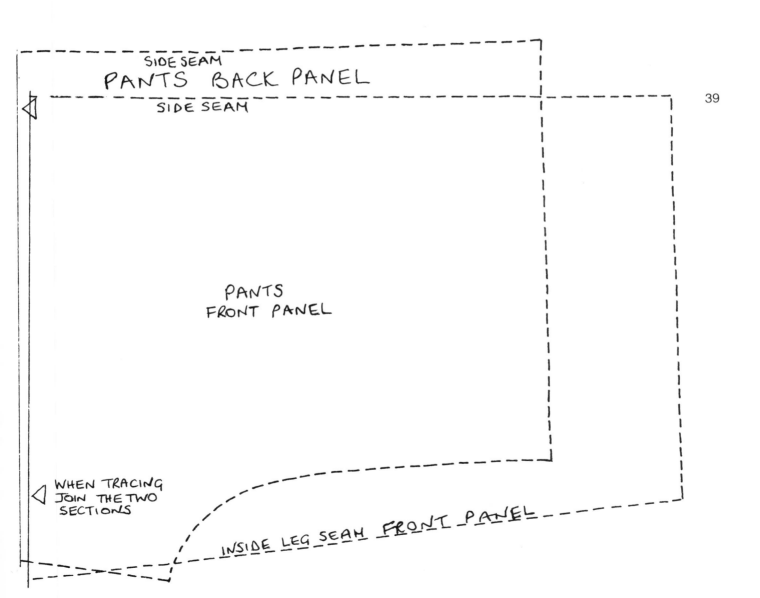

SIDE SEAM
PANTS BACK PANEL
SIDE SEAM

39

PANTS
FRONT PANEL

WHEN TRACING
JOIN THE TWO
SECTIONS

INSIDE LEG SEAM FRONT PANEL

Nightgown

model 2

Pattern pieces: front panel, back panel
Notions: bias binding

Sewing instructions:

1 Reproduce the pattern pieces on 2 x 2″ (5 x 5cm) dressmaker's pattern paper. Fold the fabric in half and pin the pieces to it, having the middle of the front and the middle front facing against the fabric fold.
2 Cut out the neckline and the lower ends of the sleeves without a seam allowance, the rest with an extra ⅜″ (1cm) for seam allowance.
3 Zigzag around the edges of all the pieces.
4 Stitch the upper arm seams.
5 Turn in and stitch the middle back seam allowances.
6 Gather the neckline and the lower ends of the sleeves until they are the same width as the doll's hand. Stitch bias binding around the neckline and the lower ends of the sleeves. Leave a loose end on both sides of the neck opening to make a tie fastening.
7 Stitch the underarm side seams and clip the seam allowance.
8 Turn in and stitch the hemline.

40

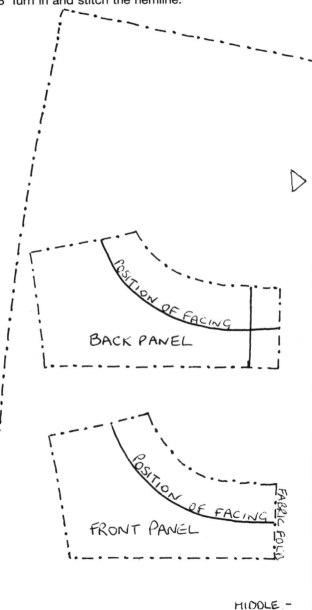

Dress   *model 3*

Pattern pieces: front panel, back panel, sleeve, front yoke, back yoke, front facing, back facing.

Notions: hook and eye fastening band, or buttons and loops, elastic.

Sewing instructions:

1 Reproduce the pattern pieces. With right sides together, fold the fabric in half and pin the pieces to it, having the front yoke, the facing of the front yoke, the sleeve and the front panel against the fabric fold.
2 Cut out the pieces with an extra ⅜" (1cm) for seam allowance. Cut out the sleeve twice.
3 Zigzag around the edges of all the pieces.
4 Gather the upper edge of the sleeves. Gather the upper edge of the front panel and both back panels.

FABRIC FOLD

41

◁ WHEN TRACING JOIN THE TWO SECTIONS

SLEEVE

GATHER

FRONT + BACK PANEL

FRONT + MIDDLE BACK _ . _ . _ (MIDDLE FRONT AGAINST FABRIC FOLD) . _ . _

5 Stitch the front panel to the front yoke.
6 Stitch the back panels to the back yokes.
7 Stitch the shoulder seams together.
8 Stitch the shoulder seams of the facings together.
9 Stitch the neckline of the front and back yoke and the neckline of the front and back facing together. Clip the seam allowance.
10 Turn in the middle of the back and stitch along the edges.
11 Turn in the facing and topstitch around the neckline.
12 Stitch pieces of hook and eye fastening band to the top of the back opening or attach buttons and loops to the back opening.
13 Stitch around the ends of the sleeves. Stitch ruched lingerie elastic ¾″ (2cm) from the ends of the sleeves.
14 Stitch the sleeves into the armholes. Clip the seam allowance.
15 Stitch the underarm side seams. Clip the curve in the seam allowance.
16 Turn in and stitch the hemline at the desired length.

Pinafore   Model 3

Pattern pieces: front panel, back panel, front yoke, back yoke, shoulder strap, pocket, armhole facings.
Notions: buttons and loops

Sewing instructions:
1 Reproduce the pattern pieces. With right sides together, fold the fabric in half and pin the pieces to it, having the middle of the front panel and the front yoke against the fabric fold.
2 Cut out the pieces with an extra ⅜″ (1cm) for seam allowance.
3 Zigzag around the edges of all the pieces.
4 Stitch the armhole facings to the front and the back panel. Clip the seam allowance.
5 Gather the upper edge of the front and back panel and stitch these to the front yoke and back yoke.
6 Stitch the pockets on where indicated.
7 Turn in and stitch the seam allowance on the neckline side of the shoulder straps.
8 Turn in and stitch the top edges of the front and the back yoke.
9 Stitch the shoulder straps to the front and the back yoke.

10 Turn in the seam allowance of the armhole (shoulder strap, yokes) and facing all together and then topstitch all the way around the armhole.
11 Turn in and stitch the seam allowance at the back. Attach buttons and loops at the top of the opening.
12 Turn in and stitch the hemline.

Pants   Model 3

Pattern pieces: pants front, pants back
Notions: ruched lingerie elastic ⅜″ (1cm) wide.

Sewing instructions:
Follow the instructions for model 1, the only variation is in step 7.
7 Turn in and stitch the seam allowance at the end of the pants legs. Stitch ruched lingerie elastic ¾″ (2cm) from the ends of the legs.

Socks   Model 1

Pattern piece: sock

Sewing instructions:
1 Reproduce the pattern piece. Fold the fabric in half and pin the piece to it, having the middle of the back against the fabric fold. For the fabric you can use an old knitted pullover.
2 Turn in and stitch the top edges.
3 Stitch the front and underneath sides.

Shoes   Model 2, 3

Pattern pieces: shoe, sole
Notions: bias binding

Sewing instructions:
1 Reproduce the pattern pieces. Lay out the pieces on a double layer of fabric (felt, plastic or fabric reinforced with fabric webbing).
2 Cut out the entire upper surface of the shoe without a seam allowance.
3 Zigzag around the edges of the pieces.
4 Stitch the back and the front part of the shoe.
5 Stitch the sole to the upper part of the shoe.
6 Stitch bias binding around all the upper edges. Leave a length hanging out on both sides of the shoe to make a tie fastening.

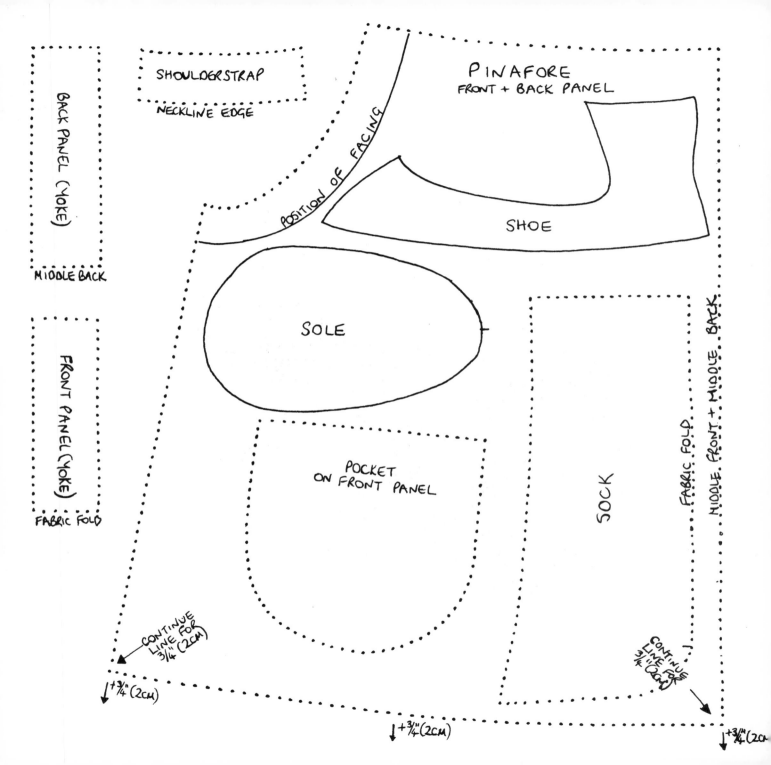

SHOULDERSTRAP

NECKLINE EDGE

BACK PANEL (YOKE)

MIDDLE BACK

FRONT PANEL (YOKE)

FABRIC FOLD

PINAFORE
FRONT + BACK PANEL

POSITION OF FACING

SHOE

SOLE

POCKET
ON FRONT PANEL

SOCK

FABRIC FOLD

MIDDLE FRONT + MIDDLE BACK

CONTINUE LINE FOR 3/4" (2CM)

↓ +3/4" (2CM)

CONTINUE LINE FOR 3/4" (2CM)

↓ +3/4" (2CM)

↓ +3/4" (2CM)

↓ +3/4" (2CM)

Stick doll
or hand puppet

Head

To make the head follow the instructions on page 18. The height of the head should be approx. 2½″ (6cm).
To make the stick doll, form the head around the stick. Then secure the head to the stick by winding thread or cord very tightly around the stick. The stick should be about 14″ (35cm) long and about ⅜″ (1cm) in diameter.
For a hand puppet, make the base of the head about 2½″ (6cm) long. Sew the inner fabric against the outer fabric. Baste three rows of elastic all the way around both fabrics, so that a cylindrical hollow is formed. A finger can be fitted into this hollow to move the head.

Hair

Follow the instructions for the other dolls' hair. You can also make a fringe (bangs) and two plaits (see diagram). Sew these on to the sides of the head. Then tie the scarf around the head and secure it to the head with a few stitches. ·
All headgear should be sewn down in this way.

Body

Pattern pieces: front, back, hand

Sewing instructions:
1 Reproduce the pattern pieces. With right sides together, fold the fabric in half and pin the pieces to it, having the front and the back against the fabric fold. The hand is not placed against the fold and is cut out twice.
2 Cut out the pieces with an extra ⅜″ (1cm) for seam allowance.
3 Zigzag around the edges of the pieces.
4 Stitch the hands on to the ends of the sleeves.
5 Stitch the upper arm seams, the hands and the side seams together. Clip the curves in the seam allowance.
6 Turn in and stitch the hemline.
7 Insert the loose fabric at the base of the neck into the neck opening. Turn in the seam allowance of the neck opening and sew this firmly to the neck threads on the head.

Cook's smock

Pattern pieces: front panel, back panel

Follow the instructions for the body, omitting the hands. Turn in and stitch the ends of the sleeves and then stitch the side seams.

Cook's hat

Pattern pieces: top section of hat, bottom section of hat

Sewing instructions:
1 Reproduce the pattern pieces. With right sides together, fold the fabric in half and pin the pieces to it, having the top section of the hat against the fabric fold.
2 Cut out the pieces with an extra ⅜″ (1cm) for seam allowance.
3 Zigzag around the edges of the pieces.
4 Gather the lower edges of the top of the hat.
5 Stitch these to the upper edges of the bottom of the hat.
6 Turn in the lower edges of the hat and stitch the side seams together.

Tunic for the cook and the gnome

Pattern pieces: front panel and back panel cut in one piece

Sewing instructions:
1 Reproduce the pattern. With right sides together, fold the fabric in half and pin the piece to it, having the upper edges against the fabric fold.
2 Cut out the side and the lower edge with an extra ⅜″ (1cm) for seam allowance and the remaining edges without a seam allowance. Zigzag around the edges.
3 Turn in and stitch the hemlines and the sides.
4 Blanket stitch around the neckline and the front edges.

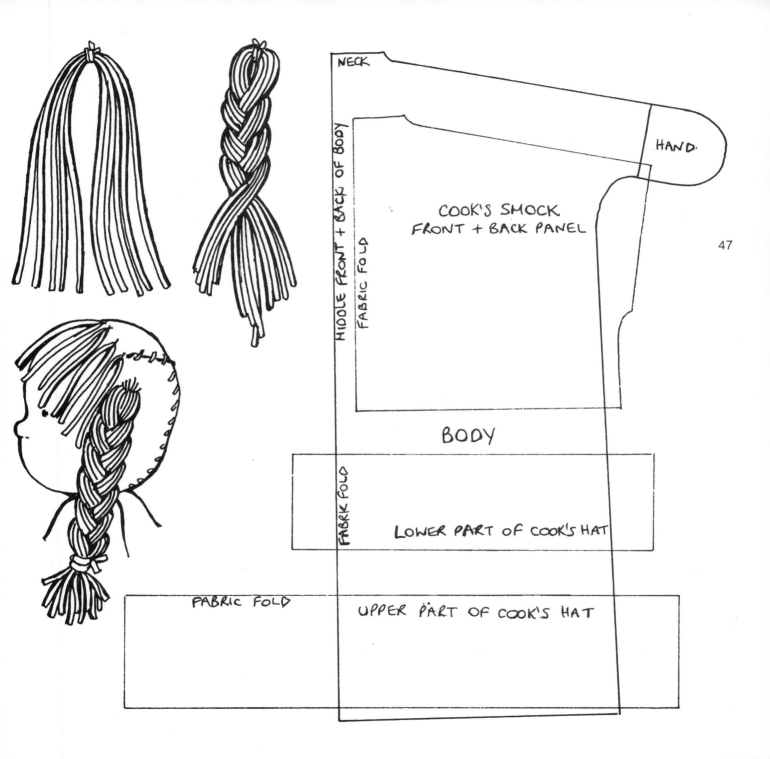

NECK

MIDDLE FRONT + BACK OF BODY

FABRIC FOLD

HAND.

COOK'S SMOCK
FRONT + BACK PANEL

47

BODY

FABRIC FOLD

LOWER PART OF COOK'S HAT

FABRIC FOLD

UPPER PART OF COOK'S HAT

Pinafore for witch (or girl)

Pattern pieces: front panel, back panel cut in one piece.

Sewing instructions
1 Reproduce the pattern. With the right sides together, fold the fabric in half and pin the pattern to it, having the top edge against the fabric fold.
2 Cut out with an extra ⅜" (1cm) for seam allowance.
3 Zigzag around the edges.
4 Clip the corners of the neckline and then turn in and stitch the seam allowance.
5 Turn in and stitch the sides and the hemline.

48
Headscarf

Sewing instructions:
1 Reproduce the pattern. With the right sides together, fold the fabric in half and pin the pattern to it with the shortest side against the fabric fold.
2 Cut out with an extra ⅜" (1cm) for seam allowance.
3 Zigzag around the edges of the scarf.
4 Cut off the corners of the seam allowance diagonally and turn in and stitch the seam allowance all the way around.

Gnome's cap

Sewing instructions:
1 Reproduce the pattern piece and pin it to single thickness fabric.
2 Cut out with an extra ⅜" (1cm) for seam allowance.
3 Zigzag around the edges.
4 Turn in and stitch the bottom edge and with right sides together stitch the seam.
5 Make a pompom (see introduction) and sew this to the tip of the cap.

FABRIC FOLD

HEADSCARF

Wings for elf or angel

Instructions:

1 Use some flexible wire that won't rust – it shouldn't be too thin. Bend the wire to make two wings.
2 Cover the wings with very thin white nylon. Do this by stretching the nylon over the wings and gathering in and stitching down the fabric at the beginning of each wing.
3 Sew the wings to the back of the puppet.

49

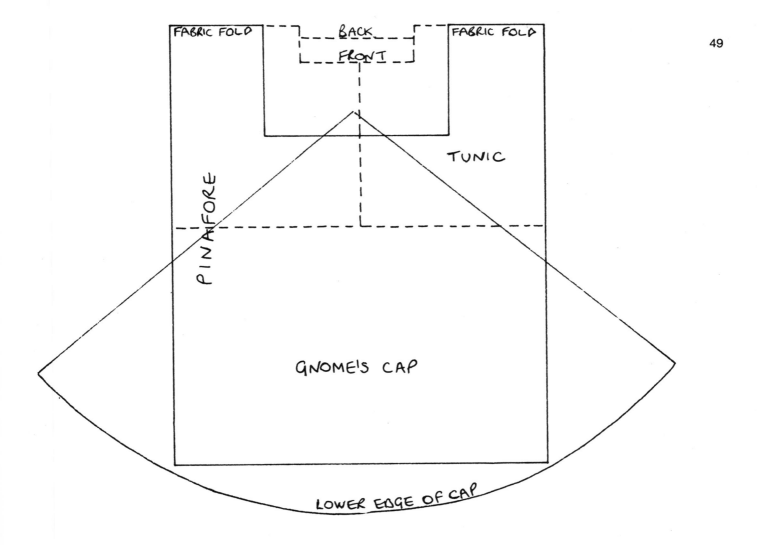

FABRIC FOLD BACK FRONT FABRIC FOLD

TUNIC

PINAFORE

GNOME'S CAP

LOWER EDGE OF CAP

Baby Dolls

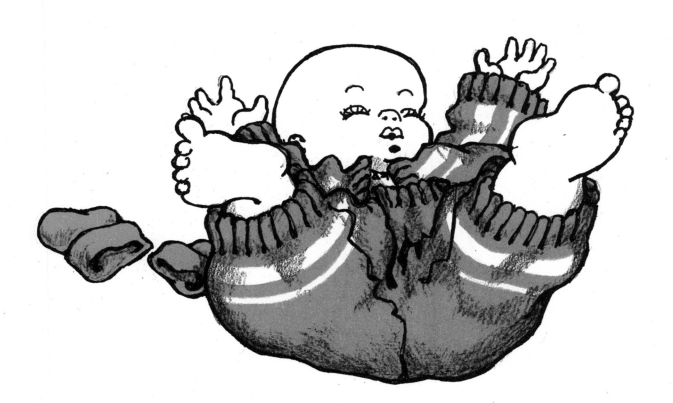

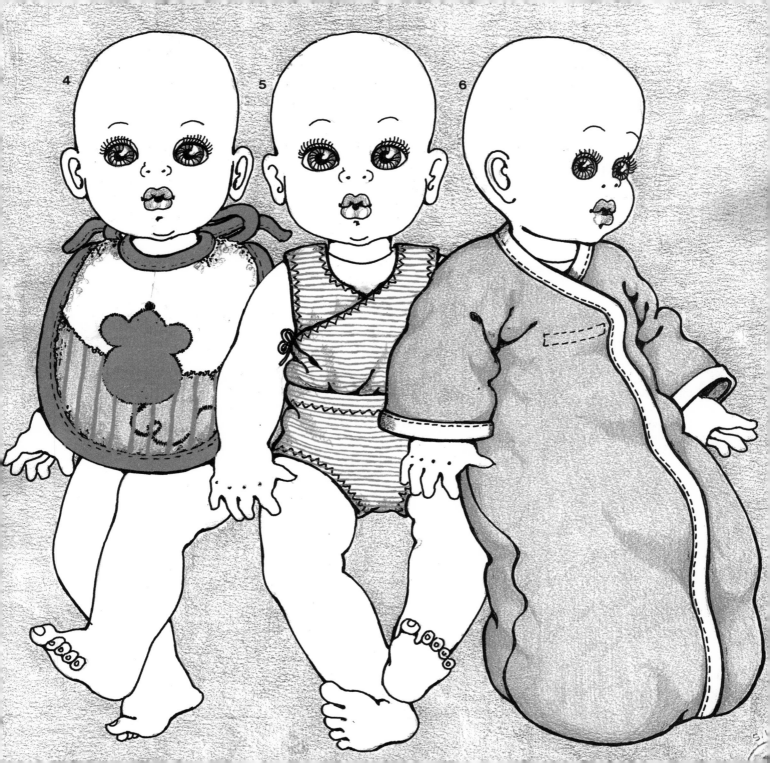

Clothes for baby dolls

Night clothes

54 **Jacket**   *model 1*

Pattern pieces: front panel, back panel
Notions: hook and eye fastening band, home-
                     knitted or shop-bought knitted cuffs,
                     bias binding.

Sewing instructions:
1 Reproduce the pattern pieces. With right sides together, fold the fabric in half and pin the pieces to it,
  having the middle of the back against the fabric fold.
  Mark the points where the pieces of hook and eye
  fastening band are to be attached.
2 Cut out the upper arm seam, the underarm side seam
  and the bottom edge of the sleeve with an extra ⅜″
  (1 cm) for seam allowance. Cut out the remaining edges
  without a seam allowance.
3 Zigzag around the eges of the pieces.
4 Stitch the upper arm seams. Press them open.
5 Stitch the cuffs to the ends of the sleeves.
6 Stitch the underarm side seams together. Clip the
  curve in the seam allowance.
7 Stitch bias binding around the edges of the jacket.
8 Stitch pieces of hook and eye fastening band where
  indicated.

Pants

Pattern pieces: pants front, pants back
Notions: ruched lingerie elastic ⅜″ (1 cm) wide.

Sewing instructions:
1 Reproduce the pattern pieces. With right sides together, fold the fabric in half and pin the pieces to it.
2 Cut out the upper edge with an extra ⅝″(1.5 cm) and

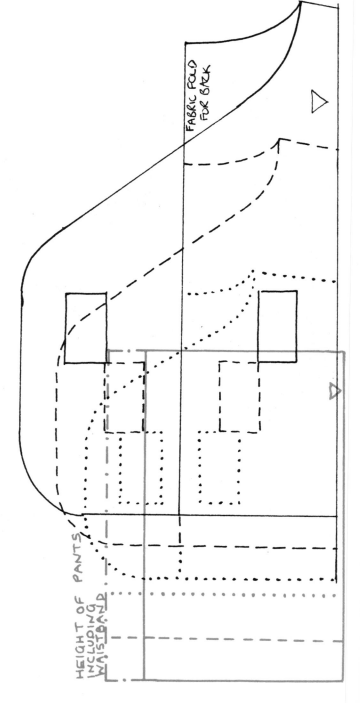

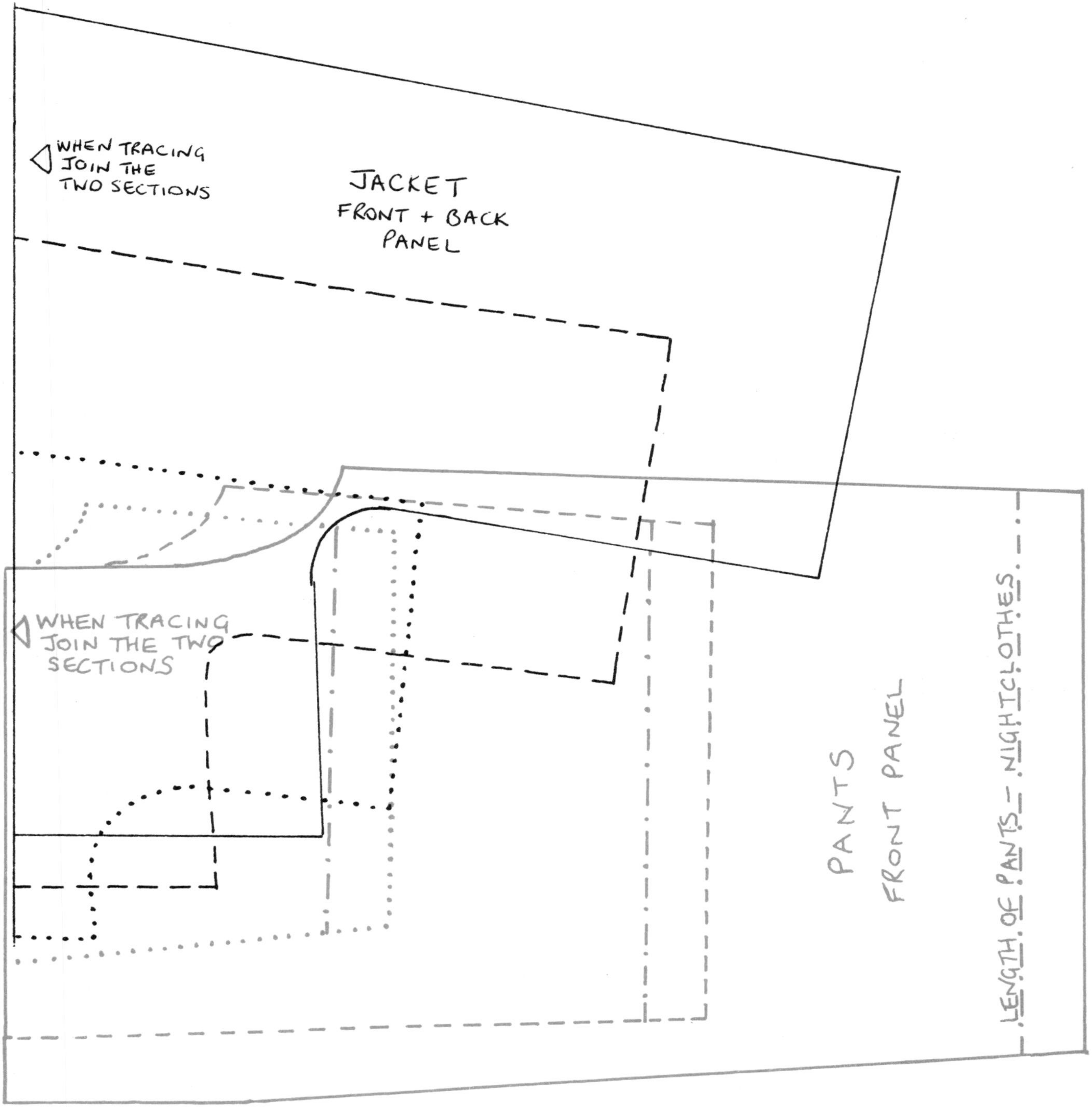

△ WHEN TRACING
JOIN THE
TWO SECTIONS

JACKET
FRONT + BACK
PANEL

55

△ WHEN TRACING
JOIN THE TWO
SECTIONS

PANTS
FRONT PANEL

LENGTH OF PANTS – NIGHTCLOTHES

remaining edges with an extra ⅜"(1cm) for seam allowance.

3 Zigzag around the edges of the pieces.
4 Stitch the inside leg seams of the pants front and the pants back together. Press the seams open.
5 Stitch the crotch seam of the front panels together. Repeat with the back panels. Clip the curve of the seam allowance. Press the seams open.
6 Turn in the seam allowance of the waist at the front and the back. Stitch stretched ruched lingerie elastic to the inside of the waist, thereby finishing the inside of the waist at the same time. To find out how much elastic is needed, measure the doll's waist with elastic. Note that you only need a piece of elastic measuring half the width of the doll's waist for the front of the pants and the same again for the back.
7 Stitch cuffs on to the ends of the legs.
8 Stitch the side seams together.

Nappy/Diaper (knitted/T-shirt fabric)   model 2

Notions: Pieces of hook and eye fastening band

Sewing instructions:
1 Reproduce the pattern piece. With right sides together fold the fabric in half and pin the piece to it. Mark the position of the hook and eye fastening band.
2 Cut out the side edge with an extra ⅝" (1.5cm) for seam allowance. The remaining edges with an extra ⅜" (1cm) for seam allowance.
3 Zigzag around the edges.
4 Turn in the seam allowance and sew it down with a zigzag stitch.
5 Stitch pieces of hook and eye fastening band where indicated.

56

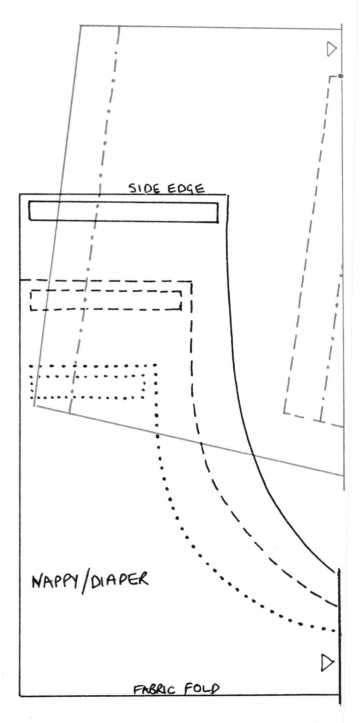

SIDE EDGE

NAPPY/DIAPER

FABRIC FOLD

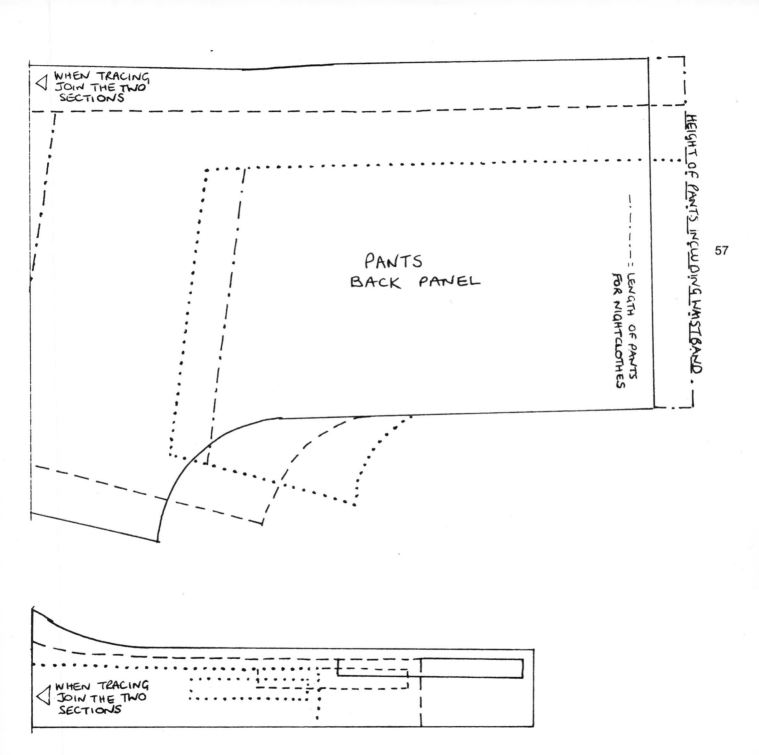

WHEN TRACING
JOIN THE TWO
SECTIONS

PANTS
BACK PANEL

= LENGTH OF PANTS
FOR NIGHTCLOTHES

HEIGHT OF PANTS INCLUDING WAISTBAND.

57

WHEN TRACING
JOIN THE TWO
SECTIONS

Bathrobe with hood model 3

Pattern pieces: bathrobe, hood
Notions: bias binding

Sewing instructions:
1 Reproduce the pieces on 2 x 2″ (5 x 5cm) dressmaker's pattern paper.
2 With right sides together, fold the fabric in half and pin the bathrobe to it, having the middle against the fabric fold. The hood is pinned to single thickness fabric.
3 Cut out the pieces without a seam allowance.
4 Finish the front of the hood with bias binding.
5 Place the hood on a corner of the bathrobe.
6 Stitch bias binding all the way around the edge of the shawl. Stitch on the hood at the same time.

Bib with applique model 4

Notions: bias binding, scraps of fabric for the applique.

Sewing instructions:
1 Reproduce the pattern.
2 With right sides together, fold the fabric in half and pin on the pattern with the middle of the front against the fabric fold.
3 Cut out the bib without a seam allowance.
4 Zigzag around the edges of the bib.
5 Reproduce the applique drawing. Cut out the pieces without a seam allowance from the scraps of material. Iron very thin fusible webbing to the backs of the pieces. First, zigzag the striped fabric to the bib. Then the mouse. Draw the tail on the bib and then zigzag stitch or embroider along the line of the tail.
6 Stitch bias binding around the edge of the bib. Begin and end at the middle of the back.
7 Finish the neckline with bias binding. Use a longer piece of bias binding than you need and leave a loose end on both sides to make a tie fastening.

Vest and panties model 5

Vest: knitted/stretch fabric

Pattern pieces: front panel, back panel
Notions: bias binding

Sewing instructions:
1 Reproduce the pattern pieces. Wtih right sides together, fold the fabric in half and pin the pieces to it, having the middle of the back against the fabric fold. Mark the positions for the tapes.
2 Cut out with an extra ⅜″ (1cm) for seam allowance.
3 Zigzag around the edges of the pieces.
4 Using a zigzag stitch, stitch the shoulder seams and the side seams, stitching on the tapes at the same time.
5 Turn in and stitch the seam allowance all the way around the edge. Stitch tapes where indicated.

Panties: knitted/stretch fabric
Notions: elastic

Sewing instructions:
1 Reproduce the pattern. With right sides together, fold the fabric in half and pin the piece to it against the fabric fold.
2. Cut out the upper edge with an extra ¾″ (2cm) for seam allowance. The remaining edges with an extra ⅜″ (1cm) for seam allowance.
3 Zigzag all the way around the edges.

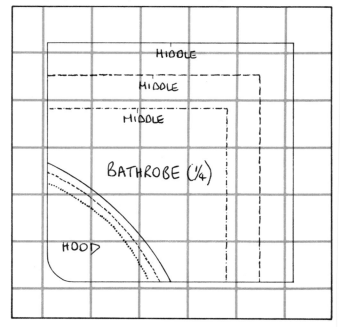

58

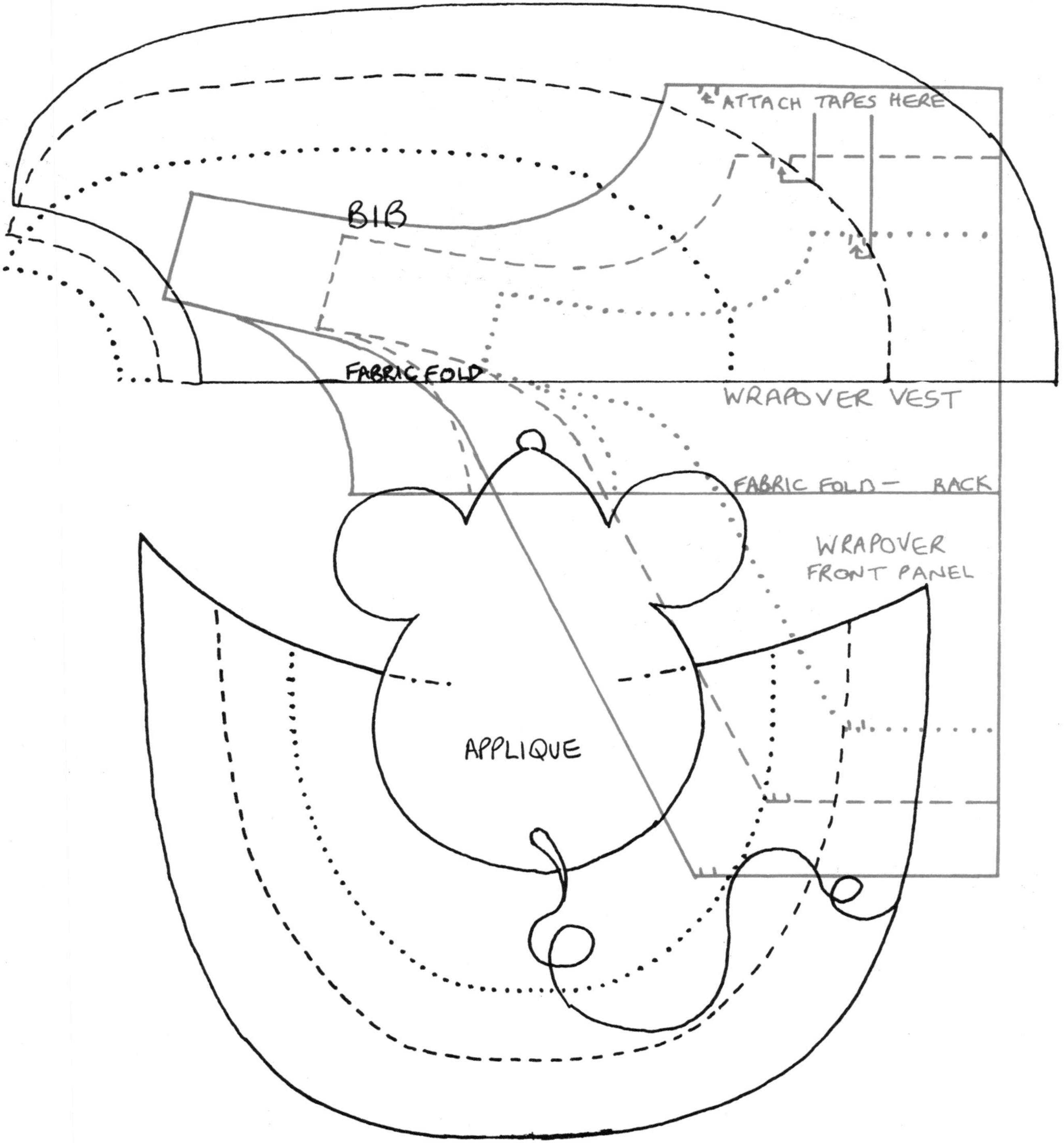

ATTACH TAPES HERE

BIB

FABRIC FOLD

WRAPOVER VEST

59

FABRIC FOLD — BACK

WRAPOVER
FRONT PANEL

APPLIQUE

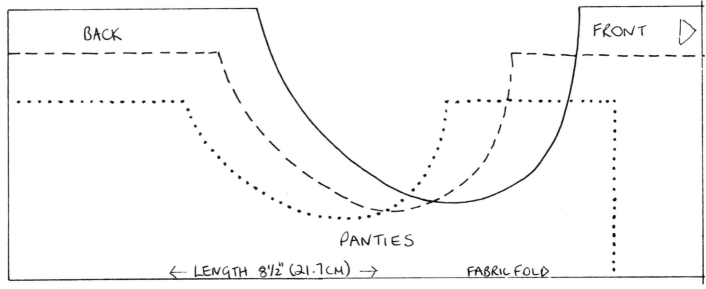

BACK

FRONT

PANTIES

← LENGTH 8½" (21.7CM) →

FABRIC FOLD

4 Turn in and stitch the seam allowance of the leg openings, using a zigzag stitch.
5 Stitch the side seams.
6 Turn in and stitch the seam allowance along the top edge. Leave a small opening for the elastic. Thread the elastic through the casing, stitch the two ends together and then stitch up the opening.

Wrapover sleeping sack　　　　　　　　　*model 6*

Pattern pieces:　front panel, back panel
Notions:　　　　bias binding

Sewing instructions:
1 Reproduce the pattern on 2 x 2" (5 x 5cm) dressmaker's pattern paper. With right sides together, fold the fabric in half and pin the pattern to it, having the middle of the back against the fabric fold.
Follow the instructions for child's sleeping sack below.

Child's wrapover sleeping sack

Pattern pieces:　front panel, back panel
Fabric needed:　36" (90cm) wide: 2⅝yd (2.4m)
　　　　　　　　54" (140cm) wide: 1¾yd (1.6m)
Notions:　　　　2½yd (2.3m) bias binding, piece of hook and eye fastening band.

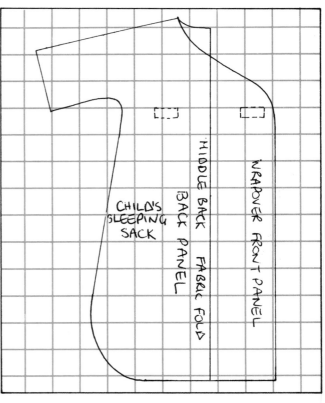

CHILD'S SLEEPING SACK

MIDDLE BACK BACK PANEL

FABRIC FOLD

WRAPOVER FRONT PANEL

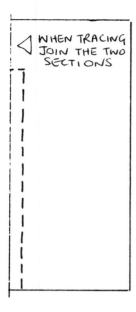

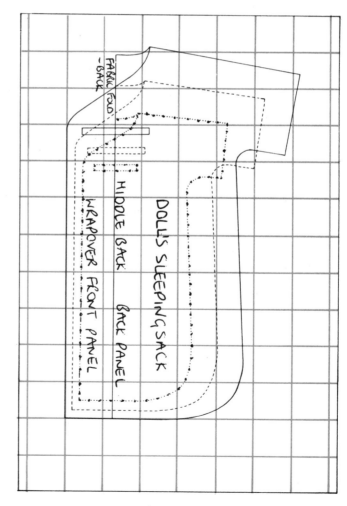

Sewing instructions:

1. Reproduce the pattern pieces on 2 x 2" (5 x 5cm) dressmaker's pattern paper.
2. With right sides together, fold the fabric in half and pin the pieces to it, having the middle of the back against the fabric fold.
3. Cut out the neckline, the upper edge and side edge of the wrapover and the bottom edge of the sleeves without a seam allowance. Cut out the other edges with an extra ⅜-¾" (1-2cm) for seam allowance.
4. Zigzag around the edges of all the pieces.
5. Stitch the upper arm seams together and press them open.
6. Stitch bias binding around the neckline and wrapover and the bottom edge of the sleeves.
7. Decide which side should wrap over on top. Stitch the underarm side seams together all the way around and stitch the bottom of the wrapover at the same time. Clip the curve in the seam allowance and press the seams open.
8. Stitch pieces of hook and eye fastening band where indicated.

Sleeveless top, pants, overalls, blouse and knitted sweater

Sleeveless top and pants

model 1

Top
Pattern pieces: front panel, back panel
Notions: bias binding and hook and eye fastening band

Sewing instructions:

1 Reproduce the pattern pieces. With right sides together, fold the fabric in half and pin the pieces to it, having the front panel against the fabric fold. Mark the points where tapes are to be sewn on.
2 Cut out the middle of the back and the shoulder seams with an extra ⅜″ (1cm) for seam allowance. The remaining edges without a seam allowance.
3 Zigzag the edges of the shoulder seams.
4 Stitch the shoulder seams.
5 Stitch bias binding around the neckline.
6 Fold in the seam allowance along the middle of the back and stitch it down. Stitch on pieces of hook and eye fastening band lengthwise to make the fastening.
7 Stitch bias binding around the edge of the garment. Fold pieces of bias binding in half and stitch around the edges to make tapes. Sew the tapes where indicated on the sides.

Pants
Pattern pieces: pants front, pants back – see pp 55-57.
Notions: ruched lingerie elastic ⅜″ (1cm) wide

Sewing instructions:

1 Reproduce the pattern pieces. With right sides together, fold the fabric in half and pin the pieces to it.
2 Cut out the top and bottom edge with an extra ⅝″

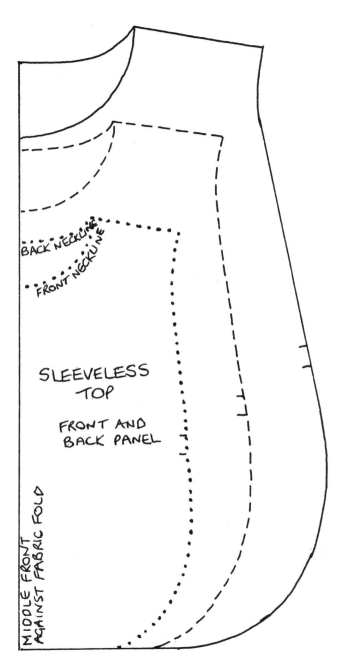

BACK NECKLINE

FRONT NECKLINE

SLEEVELESS TOP

FRONT AND BACK PANEL

MIDDLE FRONT AGAINST FABRIC FOLD

(1.5cm) for seam allowance. The remaining edges with an extra ⅜″ (1cm) for seam allowance.

3 Zigzag around the edges of the pieces.
4 Stitch the inside leg seams of the pants front and the pants back together. Press the seams open.
5 Stitch the crotch seams of the front panels together. Repeat with back panels. Clip the curve in the seam allowance. Press the seams open.
6 Turn in the seam allowance for the waist at the front and at the back. Stitch stretched ruched lingerie elastic to the inside of the waist, thereby finishing the inside of the waist at the same time. To find out how much elastic is needed, measure the doll's waist with elastic. Use a piece of elastic measuring half the width of the doll's waist for the front of the pants and the same again for the back.
7 Turn in the seam allowances at the ends of the legs. Measure the circumference of the doll's legs and stitch stretched ruched elastic to the inside.
8 Stitch the side seams together.

Overalls   model 2, 3

Pattern pieces: pants front, pants back, bib front, bib back, shoulder strap, front bib facing, back bib facing.

Notions: hook and eye fastening band or snap fasteners.

Sewing instructions:

1 Reproduce the pattern pieces. With right sides together, fold the fabric in half and pin the pieces to it, having the middle front and middle back of the bib against the fabric fold. Cut out the bibs twice. Cut out the shoulder strap twice.
2 Cut out the pieces with an extra ⅜″ (1cm) for seam allowance.
3 Zigzag around the edges of the pieces.
4 Stitch the inside leg seams of the pants front and pants back together and press the seams open.
5 Stitch the crotch seams together, clip the curve in the seam allowance and press the seam open.
6 Turn in the seam allowances at the ends of the legs. Measure the circumference of the doll's legs and stitch stretched ruched lingerie elastic to the inside.
7 Stitch the side seams together. Leave a small opening at the top.
8 Gather the top edge of the pants until both the front and back panels are the same width as the bib.
9 With right sides together, stitch the front bib to the pants front.
10 With right sides together, stitch the back bib to the pants back.
11 Fold the shoulder straps in half lengthwise and stitch along the edge. Turn them right side out and pin them with the diagonal side against the back panel.
12 With right sides together, stitch the front facing along the top edge, armholes and side of the bib. Clip the curve and the corners of the seam allowance.
13 With right sides together, stitch the back facing along the top edge, armholes and side of the back bib. At the same time, stitch in the shoulder straps being sure that these are sticking out on the right side of the fabric. Clip the curve and the corners of the seam allowance.
14 Turn the pants right side out, with the facing on the inside. Top-stitch all the way around, along the upper edge and the waistline.
15 Attach snap fasteners or stitch hook and eye fastening band where indicated.

65

BACK
FRONT
MIDDLE FRONT + BACK
BIB
FRONT + BACK PANEL
SIZE: 14" (36CM)
SHOULDER STRAP

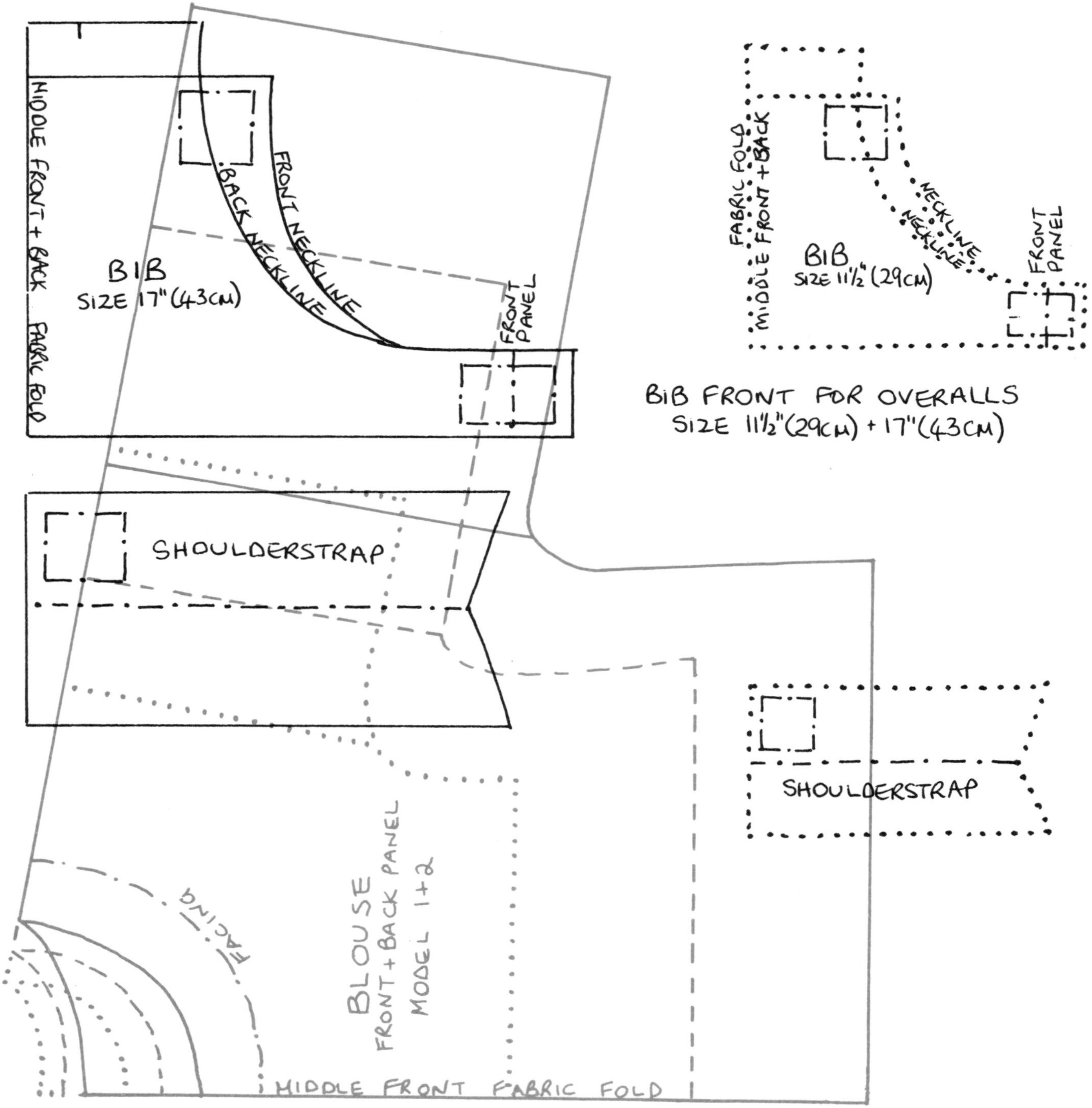

MIDDLE FRONT + BACK   FABRIC FOLD

BIB
SIZE 17"(43CM)

FRONT NECKLINE

BACK NECKLINE

FRONT PANEL

FABRIC FOLD
MIDDLE FRONT + BACK

BIB
SIZE 11½"(29CM)

NECKLINE
NECKLINE

FRONT PANEL

BIB FRONT FOR OVERALLS
SIZE 11½"(29CM) + 17"(43CM)

SHOULDERSTRAP

SHOULDERSTRAP

BLOUSE
FRONT + BACK PANEL
MODEL 1 + 2

FACING

MIDDLE FRONT FABRIC FOLD

Outdoor overalls

model 3

Pattern pieces: pants front, pants back, front bib, back bib, shoulder strap, front bib facing, back bib facing.

Notions: hook and eye fastening band or snap fasteners.

Sewing instructions:
Follow instructions for model 2
However, in this case stitch the inside leg seams and the side seams together in one go. With right sides together fit the legs into one another and stitch the crotch seams.

Blouse

model 1, 2

Pattern pieces: front panel, back panel, front neckline facing, back neckline facing.

Notions: hook and eye fastening band, ruched lingerie elastic ⅜" (1cm) wide

Sewing instructions:
1 Reproduce the pattern pieces. With right sides together, fold the fabric in half and pin the pieces to it, having the middle of the front and the middle of the front facing against the fabric fold.
2 Cut out with an extra ⅜" (1cm) for seam allowance.
3 Zigzag around the edges of all the pieces.
4 Stitch the front neckline facing to the neckline. Clip the seam allowance.
5 Stitch the back facings to the back neckline. Clip the seam allowance.
6 Stitch the upper arm seams. At the same time stitch the sides of the facings. Turn in the facing and stitch around the neckline.
7 Turn in and stitch the bottom edges of the sleeves or turn in the seam allowance at the end of the sleeves and stitch on stretched ruched lingerie elastic.
8 Stitch the underarm side seams. Clip the curve in the seam allowance.
9 Turn in and stitch the seam allowance along the bottom edge.
10 Turn in the seam allowance along the middle of the back and stitch pieces of hook and eye fastening band on to the back (see introduction).
If the neckline and the ends of the sleeves are to be finished in blanket stitch, then there is no need to cut these out with a seam allowance.

Knitted sweater: Follow instructions for model 3 page 75.

Sleeveless top with pants for your child

Size by age: 6-9 months, 18 months, 2 years
Height of child: 29" (74cm) 34" (86cm), 38" (98cm)

Sleeveless top

Pattern pieces: front panel, back panel.
Fabric needed: 36" (90cm) wide: ½yd (0.45m)
54" (140cm) wide: ½yd (0.45m)
Notions: button,
3¼yd (30m) bias binding.

Sewing instructions:
1 Reproduce the pattern pieces on 2 x 2" (5 x 5cm) dressmaker's pattern paper. Mark the pattern where tapes are to be attached.
2 With right sides together, fold the fabric in half and pin the pieces to it, having the middle of the front against the fabric fold.
3 Cut out the middle of the back and the shoulder seams with an extra ⅜-¾" (1-2cm) for seam allowance. The remaining edges without a seam allowance.
4 Zigzag around all the pieces.
5 Stitch the shoulder seams.
6 Stitch the middle back seam. Leave an opening measuring 4-6" (10-15cm) at the top.
7 Stitch bias binding around the neckline. Leave 2½" (6cm) hanging out on one side to make a loop.
8 Stitch bias binding around the edge of the garment. To make tapes, fold pieces of bias binding in half and stitch around the edges. Stitch on tapes where indicated.
9 Sew on the button opposite the loop.

67

Pants

Pattern pieces: pants front, pants back
Fabric needed: 36" (90cm) wide: 1¾yd (1.60m)
54" (140cm) wide: ⅞yd (0.80m)
Notions: ⅝yd (60cm) elastic ⅜" (1cm) wide
1¼yd (1.10m) elastic for baggy pants

Sewing instructions:

1 Reproduce the pattern pieces on 2 x 2" (5 x 5cm) dressmaker's pattern paper.

2 With right sides together, fold the fabric in half and pin the pieces to it.

3 Cut out the top edge and the bottom edge with an extra 1" (2.5cm) for seam allowance. If making baggy pants, cut out the bottom edge with an extra 3" (7cm) for seam allowance. The remaining edges with a seam allowance of ⅜-¾" (1-2cm).

4 Zigzag around the edges of the pieces.

5 Stitch the inside leg seams of the pants front and the pants back together. Press the seams open.

6 Stitch the front panel crotch seams together. Repeat with the back panels. Clip the curve in the seam allowance. Press the seam open.

7 Stitch the side seams together. Press the seams open.

8 Turn in 1" (2.5cm) along the bottom edge of the pants legs and stitch ⅝" (1.5cm) from the bottom edge. For the baggy pants leave a small opening and insert the elastic through this opening. Stitch the two ends of the elastic together and stitch up the opening.

9 Turn in 1" (2.5cm) along the top edge of the pants. Stitch along ⅝" (1.5cm) from the edge. Leave a small opening. Insert the elastic into the opening. Stitch the two ends of the elastic together and stitch up the opening.

68

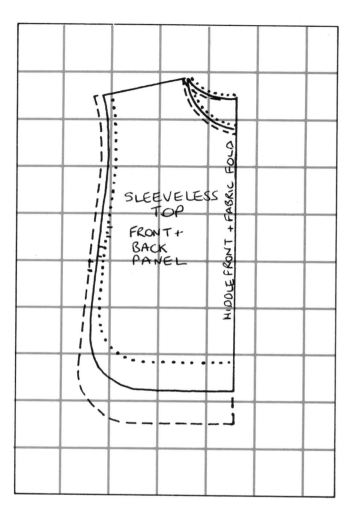

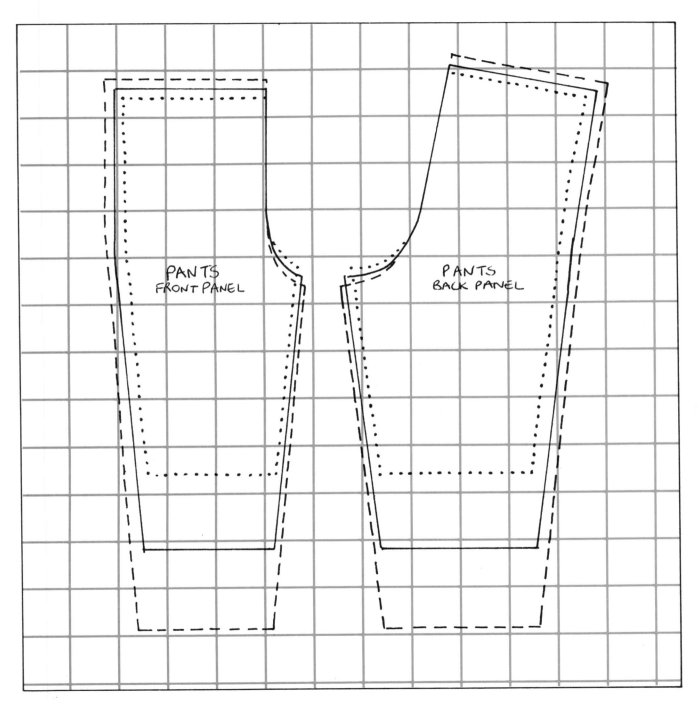

PANTS
FRONT PANEL

PANTS
BACK PANEL

69

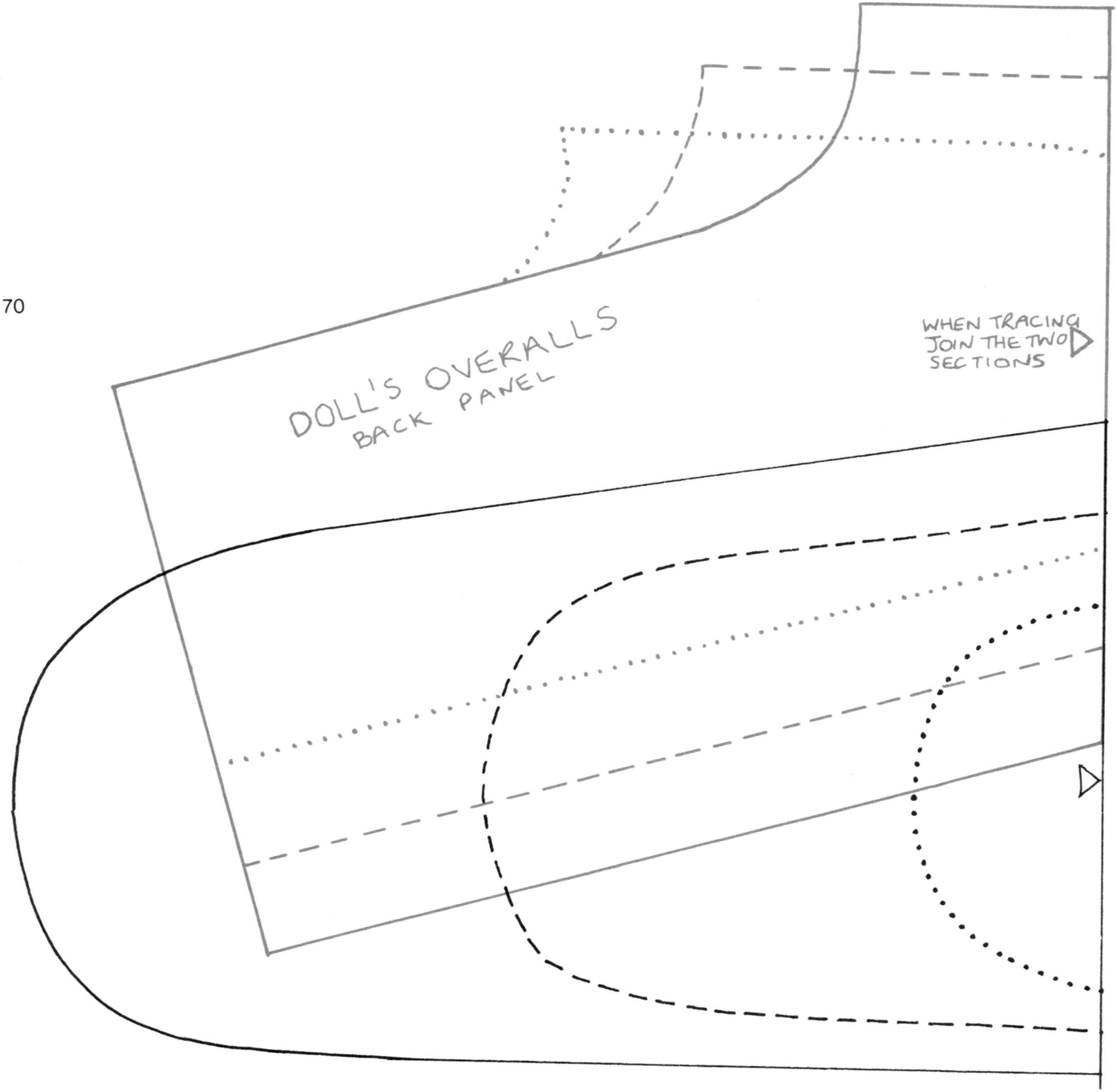

70

DOLL'S OVERALLS
BACK PANEL

WHEN TRACING
JOIN THE TWO ▷
SECTIONS

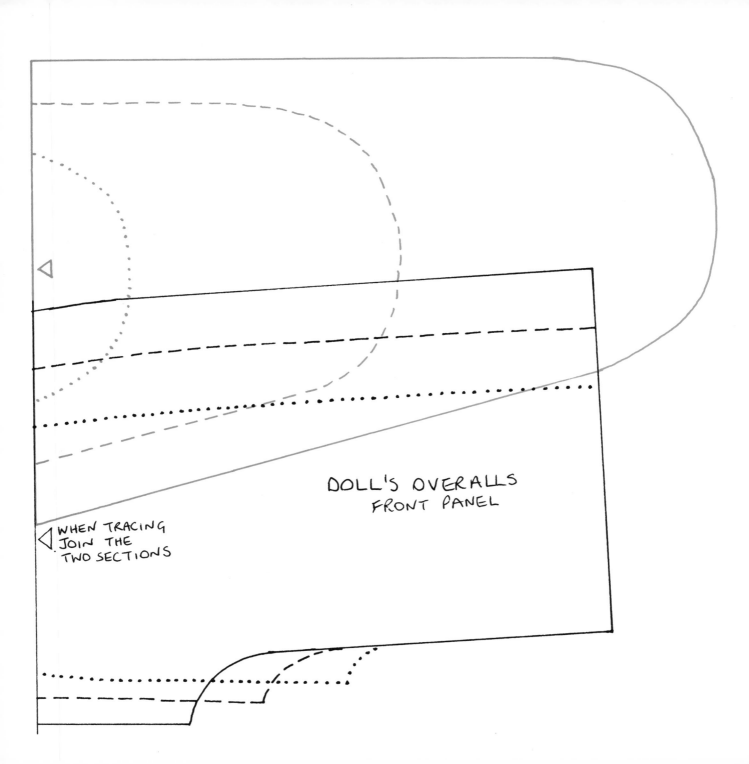

DOLL'S OVERALLS
FRONT PANEL

WHEN TRACING
JOIN THE
TWO SECTIONS

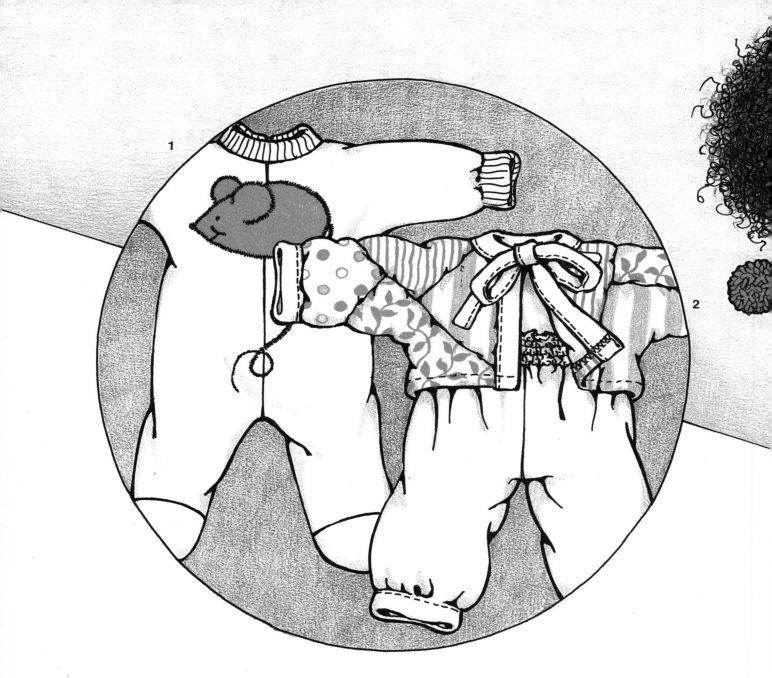

Stretch suit, pants, jacket and bolero-type jacket

Pattern pieces: front panel, back panel
Notions: bias binding

Sewing instructions:
1 Reproduce the pattern.
2 With right sides together, fold the fabric in half and pin the pieces to it, having the middle of the back against the fabric fold.

Long-sleeved stretch suit *model 1*

Pattern pieces: front panel, back panel, upper side of foot.
Notions: cuffs, hook and eye fastening band or zipper.

Sewing instructions:
1 Reproduce the pattern pieces. With right sides together, fold the fabric in half and pin the pieces to it.
2 Cut out the middle of the back with an extra 5/8″ (1.5cm) for seam allowance. The remaining edges with an extra 3/8″ (1cm) for seam allowance.
3 Zigzag around the edges of all the pieces.
4 Stitch the front foot pieces on to the front leg pieces. Clip the seam allowance and press the seams open.
5 Stitch part of the middle back seam, leaving an opening at top. Press the seam open and stitch a piece of hook and eye fastening band or a zipper into the opening. (See introduction for how to insert zipper)
6 Stitch the inside leg seams as far as the front foot pieces. Press the seams open.
7 Stitch the middle front seam and the crotch seam until it reaches the middle back seam which has already been stitched together.
8 Stitch the upper arm seams.
9 Knit or buy cuffs for the neckline and the ends of the sleeves and stitch these on with a zigzag stitch. Clip the seam allowance of the neckline.
10 Trace the drawing of the mouse and zigzag stitch it on to the front panel (see Introduction: Applique).
11 Stitch the underarm side seams and the leg seams together all the way around. Clip the curve in the seam allowance.

3 Cut out the upper arm seam and the underarm side seam with an extra ⅜" (1cm) for seam allowance. The remaining edges without a seam allowance.
4 Zigzag around the edges of all the pieces.
5 Stitch bias binding along the edge of the front opening.
6 Stitch bias binding around the neckline. Leave a piece hanging out on each side to make a tie fastening.
7 Gather the ends of the sleeves until they are the same width as the doll's hands. Finish the ends of the sleeves with bias binding.
8 Stitch the underarm side seams. Clip the curve in the seam allowance. Press the seams open.
9 Turn in and stitch the bottom edge.

Pants   model 2

Follow pattern and sewing instructions for nightclothes – pants, page 54. The only variation is in step 7.
 7 Gather the ends of the legs until they are the same width as the doll's feet and finish them with bias binding.

Knitted top   model 3

First read the section on knitting in the introduction for the stitches used and the size of knitting needles.
Cast on 24, 32, 38 stitches, according to size of doll.
Knit in plain stitch until your knitting measures ⅝" (1.5cm), 1" (2.5cm), 1¼" (3.5cm).
Increase on both sides 8, 12, 16 stitches. Keep on knitting until it measures 2¾" (7cm), 3¼" (8.5cm), 4" (10cm).
Cast off the middle 6, 10 or 12 stitches. On one side pick up the shoulder stitches on a reserve strand of yarn.
* Continue knitting on one side to a length of 3½" (9cm), 4⅛" (10.5cm), 5" (12.5cm). Now increase 4, 5, 6 stitches on the neckline side. Continue knitting to a length of 5¼" (13.5cm), 6" (15.5cm), 6¾" (17.5cm). Cast off 8, 12 or 16 stitches on the sleeve side. Continue knitting until you have a total length of 6" (15cm), 7" (18cm), 8¼" (21cm). Cast off.
Using the stitches from the reserve strand, repeat from * in reverse.
Crochet or buy a length of cord and attach pompoms to the ends (see introduction).

Stretch pants   model 3

Pattern pieces: pants front, pants back, upper side of foot .
Notions: elastic

Sewing instructions:
 1 Reproduce the pattern pieces. With right sides together fold the fabric in half and pin the pieces to it.
 2 Cut out with an extra ¾" (2cm) for seam allowance along the upper edge. The remaining edges with an extra ⅜" (1cm) for seam allowance.
 3 Zigzag around the edges of the pieces.
 4 Stitch the front foot pieces on to the front legs. Clip the seam allowance and press the seams open.
 5 Stitch the inside leg seams, the feet and the outside leg seams together all the way around. Clip the curve in the seam allowance.
 6 Turn in and stitch the seam allowance on the waistline. Leave a small opening for the elastic.
 7 Thread the elastic through the opening, stitch the ends of the elastic together and stitch up the opening.

Bolero-type jacket and pants   model 4

Bolero-type Jacket
Pattern pieces: front panel, back panel
Notions: bias binding
Sewing instructions: Follow instructions for child's bolero-type jacket below.

Pants
Pattern pieces: pants front, pants back
Notions: ruched lingerie elastic ⅜" (1cm) wide
Pattern and sewing instructions: Follow instructions for pants on page 64. See pages 70/71 for pattern.

Blouse   model 4

See pages 66 & 67 for pattern and sewing instructions

Bolero-type jacket for a child

Size by age: 9-12 months, 2 years,   4 years,
Height of child: 31" (80cm),   36" (92cm), 40" (104cm)

Pattern pieces: front panel, back panel
Fabric needed: 36" (90cm) wide: ¾yd (0.70m)
Notions: 2⅛yd (1.9m) bias binding

75

Sewing instructions:

1 Reproduce the pattern pieces on to 2 x 2" (5 x 5cm) dressmaker's pattern paper.
2 With right sides together, fold the fabric in half and pin the pieces to it. The middle back is placed against the fabric fold.
3 Cut out the middle of the front, the shoulder seams and the side seams with an extra ⅜-¾" (1-2cm) for seam allowance. The bottom edge with an extra ¾" (2cm) for seam allowance. The remaining edges without a seam allowance.
4 Zigzag around the edges of the pieces.
5 Stitch the shoulder seams. Press the seams open.
6 Stitch the side seams together. Press the seams open.
7 Turn in the bottom edge and stitch it down.
8 Turn in the front edges and stitch them down.
9 Stitch bias binding around the armholes.
10 Stitch bias binding around the neckline. Use 24" (60cm) more bias binding than you need for the neckline and leave 12" (30cm) hanging out on both sides to make a tie fastening.

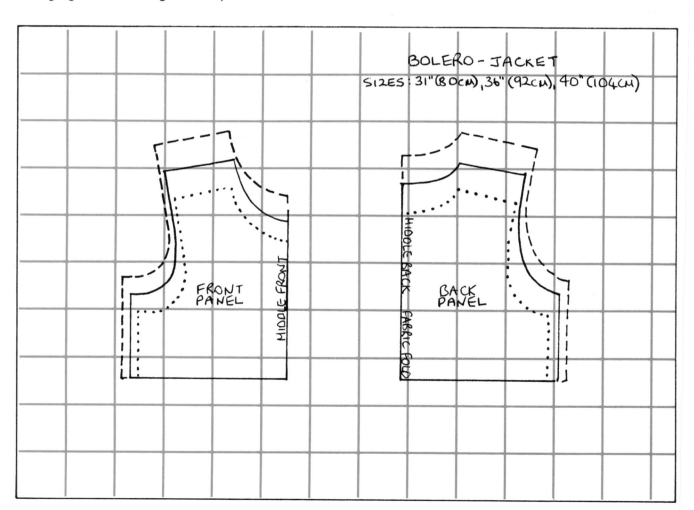

BOLERO - JACKET
SIZES: 31" (80CM), 36" (92CM), 40" (104CM)

FRONT PANEL

MIDDLE FRONT

BACK PANEL

MIDDLE BACK FABRIC FOLD

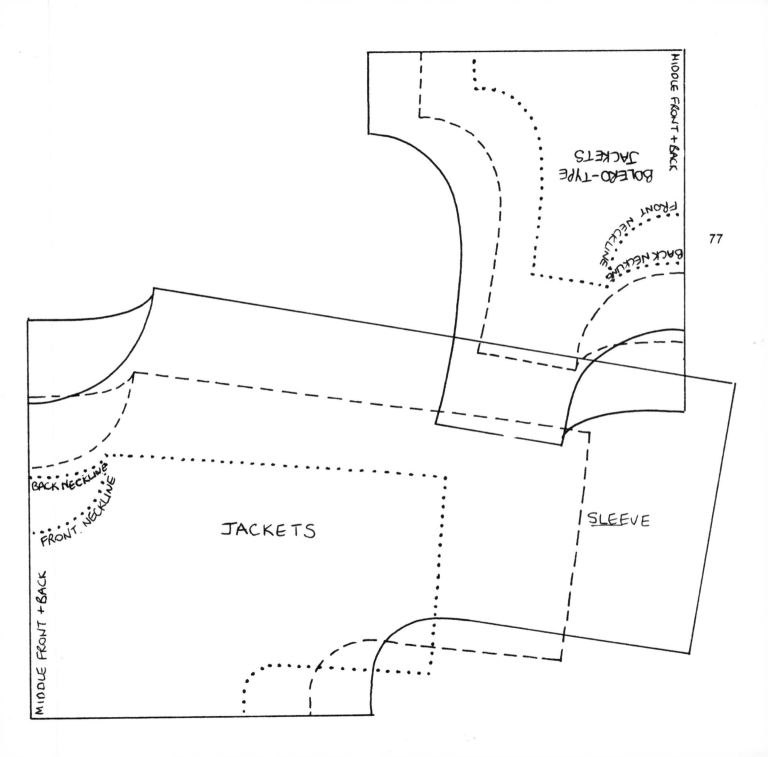

BOLERO-TYPE JACKETS

MIDDLE FRONT + BACK

FRONT NECKLINE

BACK NECKLINE

77

SLEEVE

BACK NECKLINE

FRONT. NECKLINE

JACKETS

MIDDLE FRONT + BACK

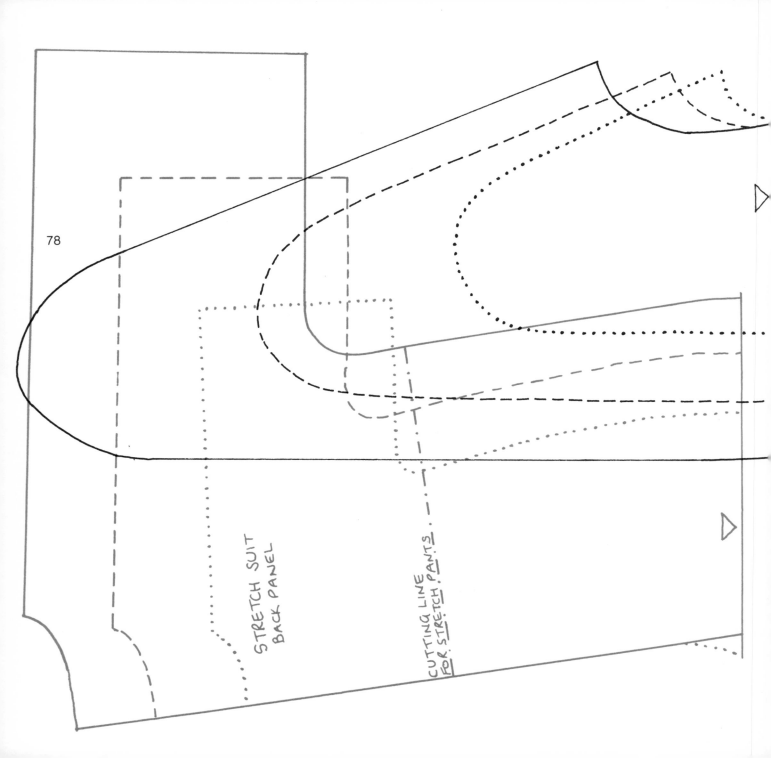

78

STRETCH SUIT
BACK PANEL

CUTTING LINE
FOR STRETCH PANTS

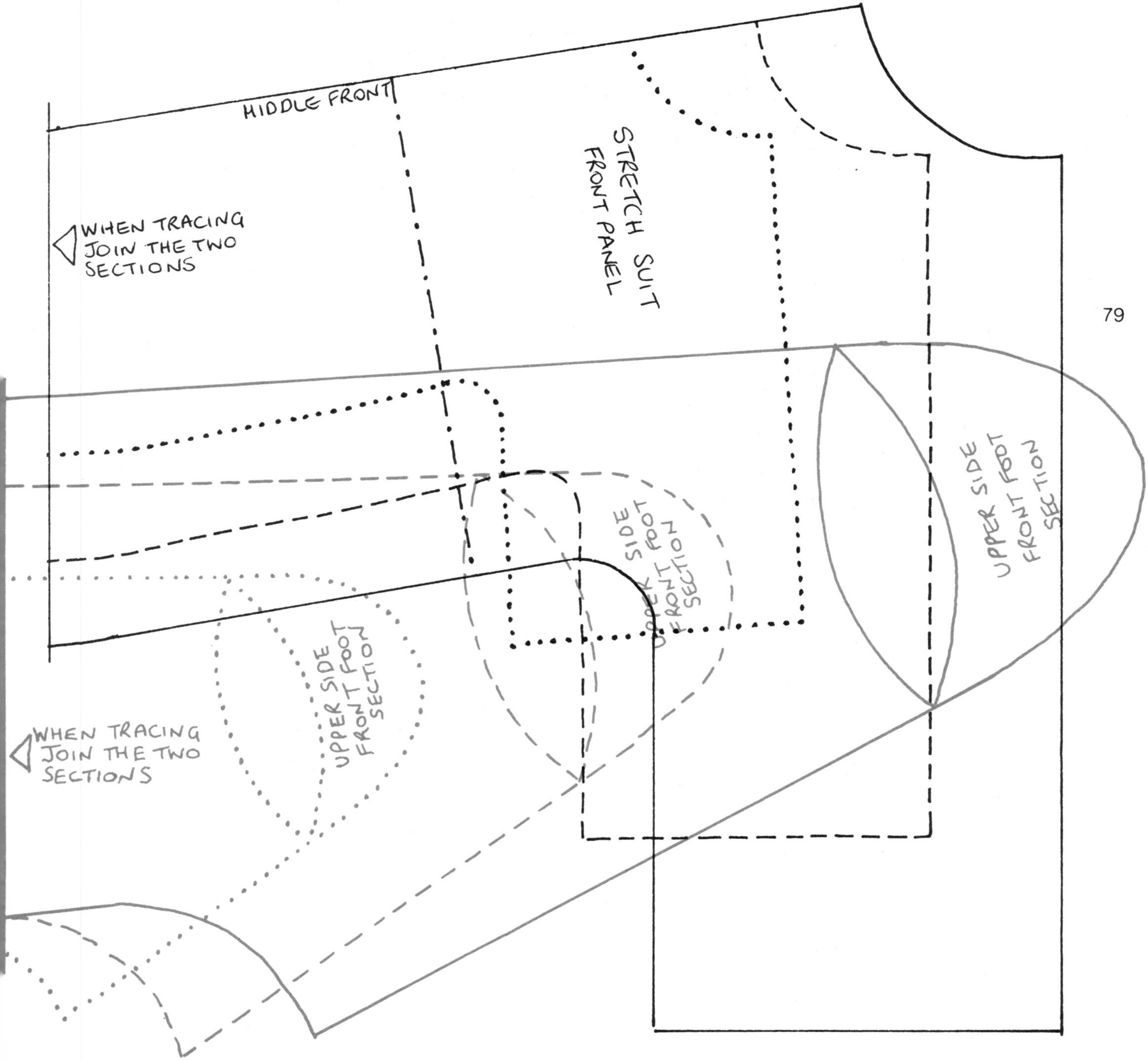

MIDDLE FRONT

WHEN TRACING
JOIN THE TWO
SECTIONS

STRETCH SUIT
FRONT PANEL

79

UPPER SIDE
FRONT FOOT SECTION

UNDER SIDE
FRONT FOOT
SECTION

UPPER SIDE
FRONT FOOT
SECTION

WHEN TRACING
JOIN THE TWO
SECTIONS

Dresses and pinafores

Dress *model 1, 2*

Pattern pieces: front panel, back panel, sleeve, front yoke, back yoke, front facing, back facing.

Notions: hook and eye fastening band, elastic.

Sewing instructions:
1 Reproduce the pattern pieces. With right sides together, fold the fabric in half and pin the pieces to it. Place the front yoke, the front yoke facing, the sleeve and the front panel against the fabric fold. Cut out the sleeve twice.
2 Cut out with an extra ⅜″ (1cm) for seam allowance.
3 Zigzag around the edges of all the pieces.
4 Gather the sleeves along the upper edge. Gather the front panel and the two back panels along the top edge until they measure the same width as the front and the back yoke.
5 Stitch the front panel to the front yoke.
6 Stitch the back panels to the back yokes.
7 Stitch the shoulder seams together.
8 Stitch the shoulder seams of the facings together.
9 Stitch the neckline of the front and back yoke and the neckline of the front and back facing together. Clip the seam allowance.
10 Turn in the middle of the back and stitch the edges.
11 Turn in the facing and top-stitch around the neckline.
12 Stitch pieces of hook and eye fastening band to the top of the back opening or attach buttons and loops.
13 For Model 2, turn in and stitch the bottom edge of the sleeves. For Model 1, do a second row of stitching to make a casing. Leave a small opening. Insert elastic through the opening and stitch the two ends together. Stitch up the opening.
14 Stitch the sleeves into the armholes. Clip the seam allowance.
15 Stitch the underarm side seams. Clip the curve in the seam allowance.
16 Stitch the hemline at the desired length.

Pinafore *model 1, 3, 4 and 5*

Pattern pieces: front panel, back panel, front yoke, back yoke, front facing, back facing, frill, armhole facing.

Notions: hook and eye fastening band or buttons and loops, lace (optional)

Sewing instructions:
1 Reproduce the pattern pieces. With right sides together, fold the fabric in half and pin the pieces to it. The front panel, front yoke frill and armhole facing are placed against the fabric fold. Cut out the frill and armhole facing twice.
2 Cut out the pieces with an extra ⅜″ (1cm) for seam allowance.
3 Zigzag around the edges of all the pieces.
4 Gather the frills between the points indicated on the pattern.
5 Stitch the side seams.
6 Stitch the armhole facings to the armholes. Clip the seam allowance. Turn the facing to the inside of the dress and press.
7 Gather the top edges of the front panel and the two back panels until they are the same width as the front and the back yoke.
8 Stitch the front panel to the front yoke.
9 Stitch the back panels to the back yokes.
10 Stitch the shoulder seams together.
11 Stitch the shoulder seams of the facings together.
12 Stitch the neckline of the front and back yoke and the neckline of the front and back facing together. Clip the seam allowance.
13 Turn in the middle back seams and stitch along the edges.
14 Turn the facing to the inside and top-stitch around the neckline.
15 Turn in and stitch the outer edge of the frills.
16 Stitch the frills to the armholes on the front panel and the back panel.
17 Turn in the seam allowance on the frill. Turn in the seam allowance on the side edges of the front yoke facing and the back yoke facing. Stitch around the

armhole. In doing so, stitch the lower edge of the frills on to the front and back panel.

18 Turn in and stitch the bottom edge.
19 Stitch hook and eye fastening band or buttons and loops to the opening in the middle of the back yoke.

In model 5, the frill is omitted.
In model 1, decorative braid or lace is stitched to the outer edge of the frill and the hemline of the pinafore.

Sundress
model 6

Pattern pieces: front panel, back panel
Notions: ruched lingerie elastic ⅜″ (1cm) wide, bias binding

Sewing instructions:
1 Reproduce the pattern pieces. With right sides together, fold the fabric in half and pin the pieces to it, having the middle of the front and the middle of the back against the fabric fold.
2 Cut out the armholes without a seam allowance. The remaining edges with an extra ⅜″ (1cm) for seam allowance.
3 Zigzag around the edges of all the pieces.
4 Stitch the side seams.
5 Turn in and stitch the bottom edge.
6 Fold in the top edge of the front panel and stitch stretched ruched lingerie elastic to the inside.
7 Fold in the top edge of the back panel and stitch stretched ruched lingerie elastic to the inside.
8 Stitch bias binding around the armholes. Leave a long piece of tape hanging out on both sides to make a tie fastening on the shoulders.

Skirt or Petticoat
model 2

Pattern pieces: front panel, back panel
Notions: elastic

Sewing instructions:
1 Reproduce the pattern pieces. With right sides together, fold the fabric in half and pin the pieces to it, having the middle of the front and the middle of the back against the fabric fold.
2 Cut out the top edge with an extra ¾″ (2cm) for seam allowance, the remaining edges with an extra ⅜″ (1cm) for seam allowance.
3 Zigzag around the edges of all the pieces.

4 Stitch the side seams.
5 Turn in and stitch the bottom edge.
6 Turn in and stitch the seam allowance along the top edge. Leave a small opening for the elastic.
7 Insert the elastic into the casing. Stitch the ends of elastic together and stitch up the opening.

Matching pantaloons, pantaloons with lace edging
model 1, 4 and 6

Use pattern for pants on pages 55 and 57 and follow sewing instructions for pants on page 64.
For the lace-edged pantaloons cut the legs shorter and instead of elastic, stitch lace to the bottom edge of the legs.

83

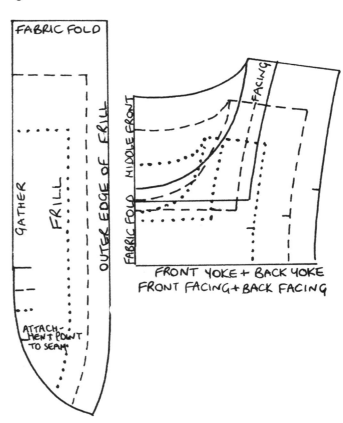

FRONT YOKE + BACK YOKE
FRONT FACING + BACK FACING

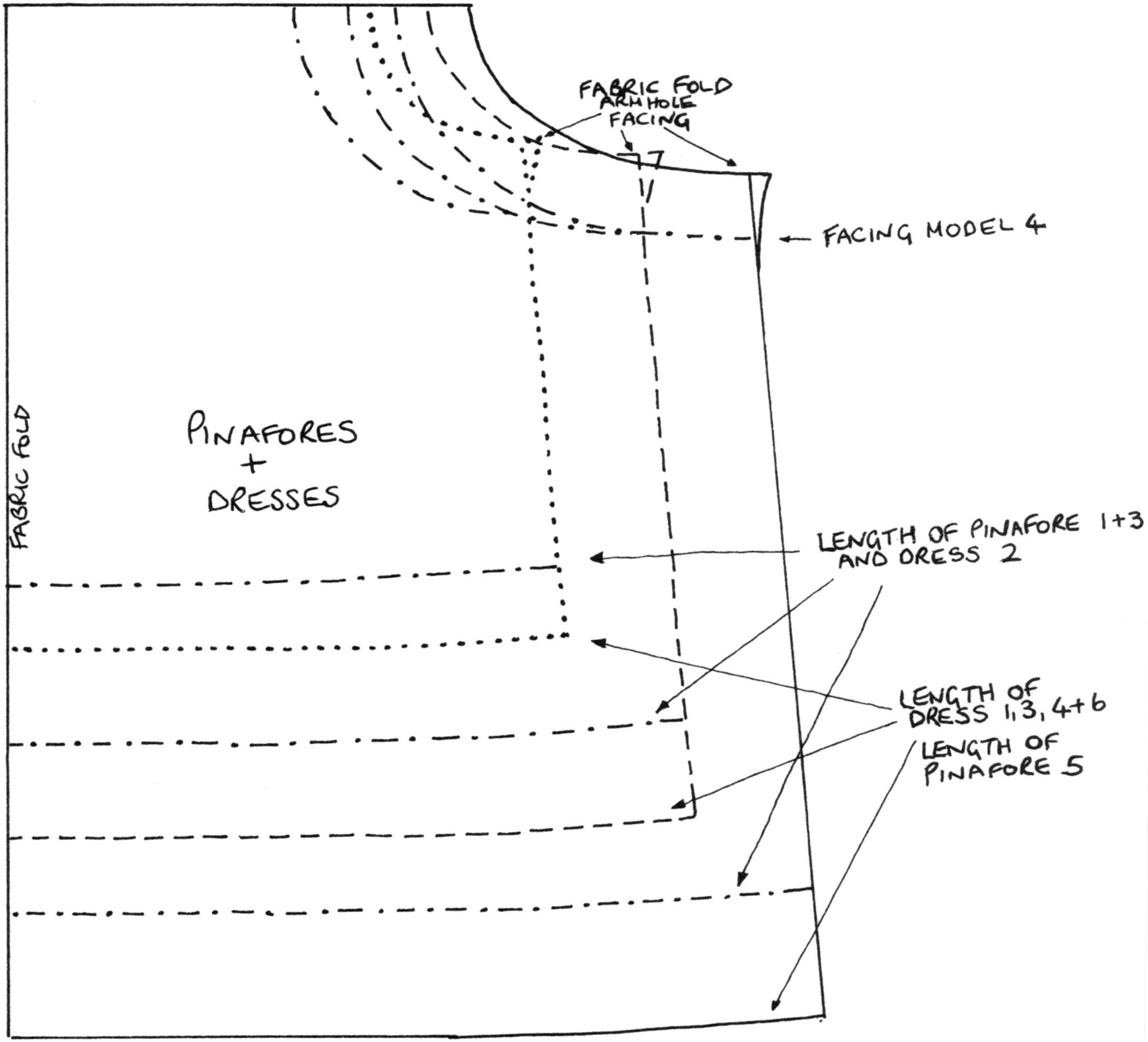

FABRIC FOLD
ARM HOLE
FACING

← FACING MODEL 4

FABRIC FOLD

PINAFORES
+
DRESSES

84

LENGTH OF PINAFORE 1+3
AND DRESS 2

LENGTH OF
DRESS 1,3,4+6

LENGTH OF
PINAFORE 5

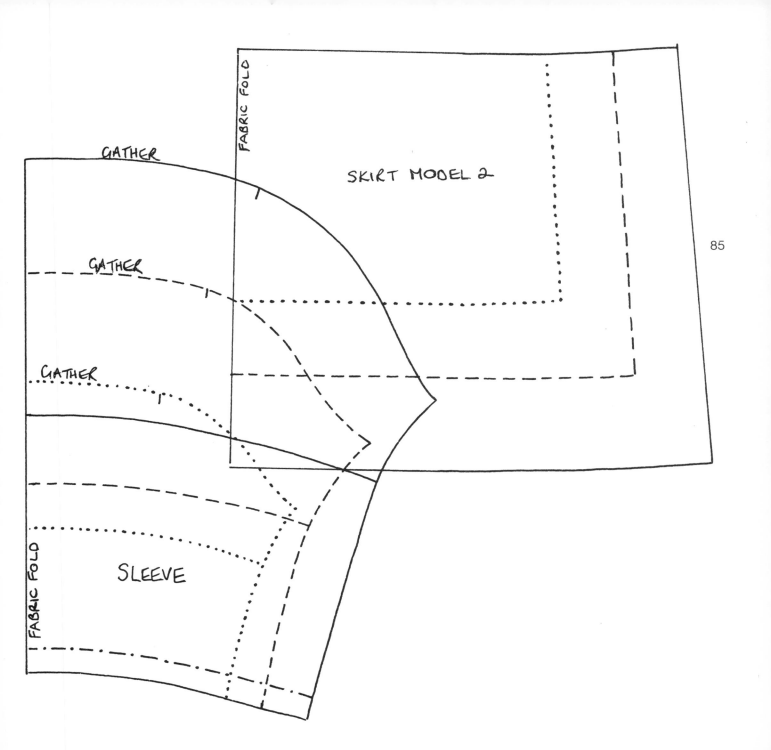

FABRIC FOLD

SKIRT MODEL 2

85

GATHER

GATHER

GATHER

FABRIC FOLD

SLEEVE

Dress for your child   *model 2*

Size by age: *2 years,   4 years,   6 years*
Height of child: *38" (92cm), 40" (104cm), 45" (116cm)*
Pattern pieces: front panel, back panel, front yoke, back
yoke, front facing, back facing, sleeve.
Fabric needed: 36" (90cm) wide: 2¾yd (2.5m)
54" (140cm) wide: 1¾yd (1.6m)
Notions: 12" (30cm) zipper

Sewing instructions:

 1 Reproduce the pattern pieces on 2 x 2" (5 x 5cm)
    dressmaker's pattern paper.
 2 With right sides together, fold the fabric in half and
    pin the pieces to it, having the middle front of the front
    yoke, the middle front of the front panel and the sleeve
    against the fabric fold.
 3 Cut out the pieces with an extra ⅜-¾" (1-2cm) for
    seam allowance. The bottom edge with an extra 1⅛"
    (3cm) for seam allowance.
 4 Zigzag around the edges of all the pieces.
 5 Gather the sleeves along the top edge. Gather the
    front panel and the back panels along the top edge.
 6 Stitch the back panels to the back yokes.
 7 Stitch the front panel to the front yoke.
 8 Stitch the middle back seam as far as the mark indi-
    cated on the pattern.
 9 Stitch the shoulder seams together.
10 Stitch the sleeves into the armholes. Clip the curve in
    the seam allowance.
11 Stitch the underarm side seams. Clip the curve in the
    seam allowance.
12 Stitch the zipper into the opening in the back seam.
    (See introduction for how to insert zipper.)
13 Stitch the shoulder seams of the front and the back
    facing.
14 With right sides together stitch the neckline of the
    front and back yoke and the neckline of the front and
    back facing together. Clip the seam allowance. Turn
    in the facing and top-stitch around the edge of the
    neckline. On the inside, sew the facing to the shoulder
    seams and to the edge of the zipper.
15 Turn in and stitch the bottom edge of the sleeves.
16 Turn in and stitch the bottom edge of the dress.

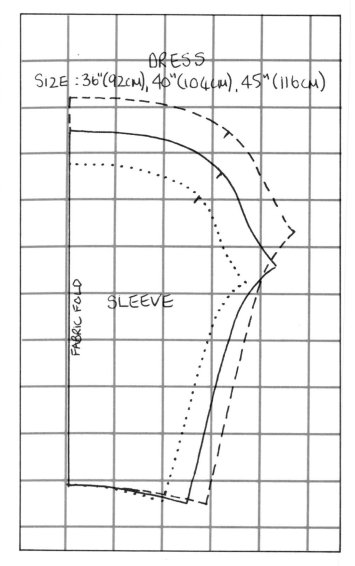

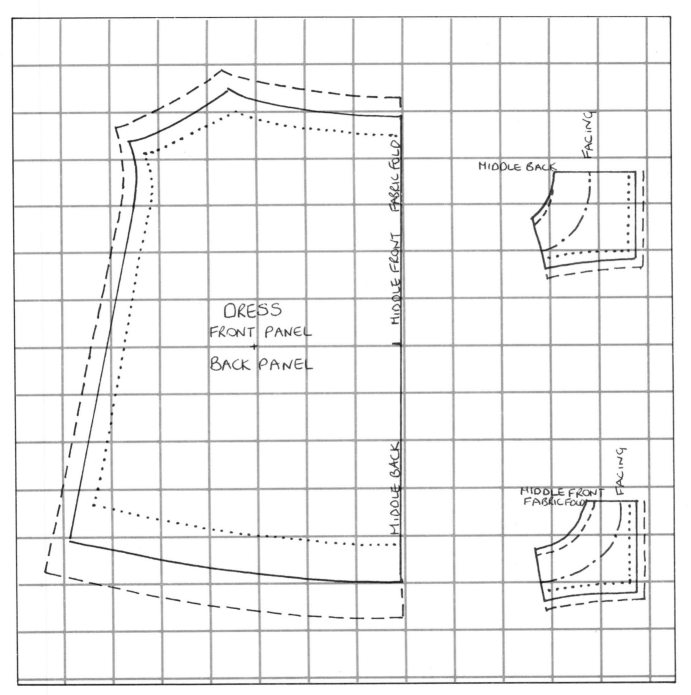

DRESS
FRONT PANEL
+
BACK PANEL

MIDDLE FRONT FABRIC FOLD

MIDDLE BACK

MIDDLE BACK

FACING

MIDDLE FRONT
FABRIC FOLD

FACING

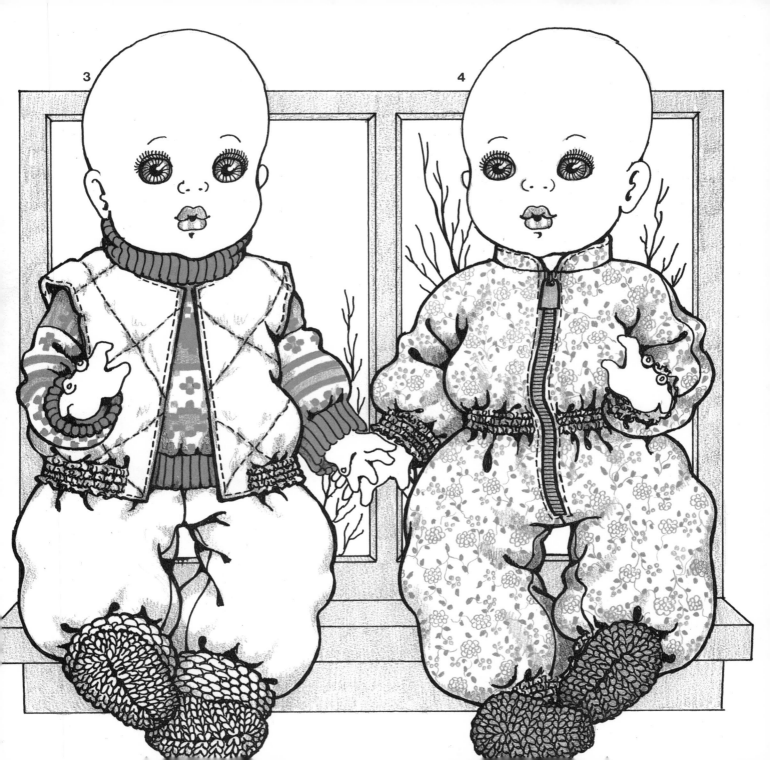

Outdoor suits, pants, sleeveless jacket or bodywarmer and sweater

90 **Outdoor all-in-one suit with hood** *model 1*

Pattern pieces: front panel, back panel, hood, casing
Notions: zipper, cord, cuffs

Sewing instructions:

1 Reproduce the pattern pieces. With right sides together, fold the fabric in half and pin the pieces to it having the casing against the fabric fold. Mark the position of the zipper on the middle of the front. Mark the position of the casing.
2 Cut out the middle of the front with an extra ⅝" (1.5cm) for seam allowance. The remaining edges with an extra ⅜" (1cm) for seam allowance. Cut out the hood once again in lining fabric.
3 Zigzag around the edges of all the pieces.
4 Stitch the inside leg seams.
5 Stitch the crotch seam as far as the mark in the middle of the front. Clip the curve in the seam allowance.
6 Stitch the upper arm seams.
7 Knit or buy cuffs and stitch these to the ends of the sleeves and legs.
8 Stitch the underarm side seams. Clip the curve in the seam allowance.
9 Turn in and press the seam allowance of the casing and stitch this on where indicated.
10 Stitch the zipper into the middle of the front seam. (See introduction for how to insert zipper.)
11 Stitch the hood sections together. Stitch the hood to the neckline.
12 Stitch the lining sections of the hood together.
13 With right sides together, stitch the front edges of the hoods together and turn the lining to the inside.
14 Clip the seam allowance of the neckline. Press the seam allowance of the hood neckline and the seam allowance of the garment neckline up. Stitch the neckline of the hood lining to the neckline of the garment.
15 Thread a cord through the casing and attach pompoms (see introduction) to the ends of the cord.

Hooded jacket *model 2*

Pattern pieces: front panel, back panel, hood
Notions: hook and eye fastening band, ruched lingerie elastic ⅜" (1cm) wide

Sewing instructions:

1 Reproduce the pattern pieces. With right sides together, fold the fabric in half and pin the pieces to it, having the middle of the back against the fabric fold. Mark the position of the hook and eye fastening band.
2 Cut out the middle of the front with an extra ⅝" (1.5cm) for seam allowance. The remaining edges with a seam allowance of ⅜" (1cm). Cut out the hood again in lining fabric.
3 Zigzag around the edges of all the pieces.
4 Stitch the upper arm seams.
5 Turn in the seam allowance at the bottom edge of the sleeves and stitch stretched ruched lingerie elastic to the inside.
6 Stitch the underarm side seams and clip the curve in the seam allowance.
7 Turn in the bottom edge of the jacket and stitch stretched ruched lingerie elastic to the inside. First measure the hip width of the doll.
8 Stitch the hood sections together. Clip the seam allowance.
9 Stitch the hood lining sections together. Clip the seam allowance.
10 With right sides together stitch the front edges of the hoods together. Turn the lining to the inside.
11 Stitch the neckline of both hoods to the neckline of the jacket. Stitch as far as the middle of the front.
12 Trim the seam allowance on the neckline as narrow as possible and, starting ⅜" (1cm) from the middle of the front, zigzag or blanket stitch it down.
13 Turn in the seam allowances on the edges of the front opening. Stitch hook and eye fastening band where indicated.

Outdoor pants
model 2

Pattern pieces: pants front, pants back
Notions: elastic

Pattern and sewing instructions: use pattern and follow instructions for outdoor overalls, omitting bib front, on page 67.

Sleeveless jacket or bodywarmer
model 3

Pattern pieces: front panel, back panel
Notions: ruched lingerie elastic ⅜" (1cm) wide

Sewing instructions:
1 Reproduce the pattern pieces. With right sides together, fold the fabric in half and pin the pieces to it, having the middle of the back against the fabric fold.
2 Cut out the pieces with an extra ⅜" (1cm) for seam allowance.
3 Zigzag around the edges of all the pieces.
4 Stitch the shoulder seams.
5 Clip the armhole seam allowance and turn in and stitch.
6 Stitch the side seams.
7 Turn in the seam allowance along the bottom edge and stitch stretched ruched lingerie elastic to the inside of the jacket.
8 Clip the neckline seam allowance and turn in and stitch.
9 Turn in the seam allowances along the middle of the front and stitch them down.

Pants
model 3

Pattern pieces: pants front, pants back
Notions: ruched lingerie elastic ⅜" (1cm) wide

Pattern and sewing instructions: use pattern and follow instructions for pants (model 1) page 64.

All-in-one suit with stand-up collar
model 4

Pattern pieces: front panel, back panel, collar, collar facing
Notions: zipper, ruched lingerie elastic ⅜" (1cm) wide.

Sewing instructions:
1 Reproduce the pattern pieces. With right sides together, fold the fabric in half and pin the pieces to it, having the collar and the collar facing against the fabric fold. Mark the position of the zipper on the middle of the front. Mark the position of the ruched lingerie elastic at the waist.
2 Cut out the middle of the front with an extra ⅝" (1.5cm) for seam allowance. The remaining edges with an extra ⅜" (1cm) for seam allowance.
3 Zigzag around the edges of all the pieces.
4 Stitch the inside leg seams.
5 Stitch the crotch seam as far as the mark for the zipper in the middle of the front. Clip the curve in the seam allowance.
6 Stitch the upper arm seams.
7 Turn in the bottom edge of the sleeves and stitch stretched ruched lingerie elastic to the inside.
8 Turn in the bottom edge of the legs and stitch stretched ruched lingerie elastic to the inside.
9 Stitch the underarm side seams and clip the curve in the seam allowance.
10 Stitch ruched lingerie elastic where indicated around the waistline.
11 Stitch the zipper into the middle of the front seam. (See introduction for how to insert zipper.)
12 With right sides together pin the collar to the neckline of the garment and stitch all the way around.
13 With right sides together pin the collar facing to the right side of the collar and stitch all the way around the top edge. Clip the curve in the seam allowance. Turn right side out.
14 Clip the seam allowance of the neckline. Fold the seam allowances of the neckline and the collar facing into the inside of the collar and stitch the facing to the neckline.
15 Top-stitch along the top of the collar as far as the stitching on the zipper.

STAND-UP COLLAR

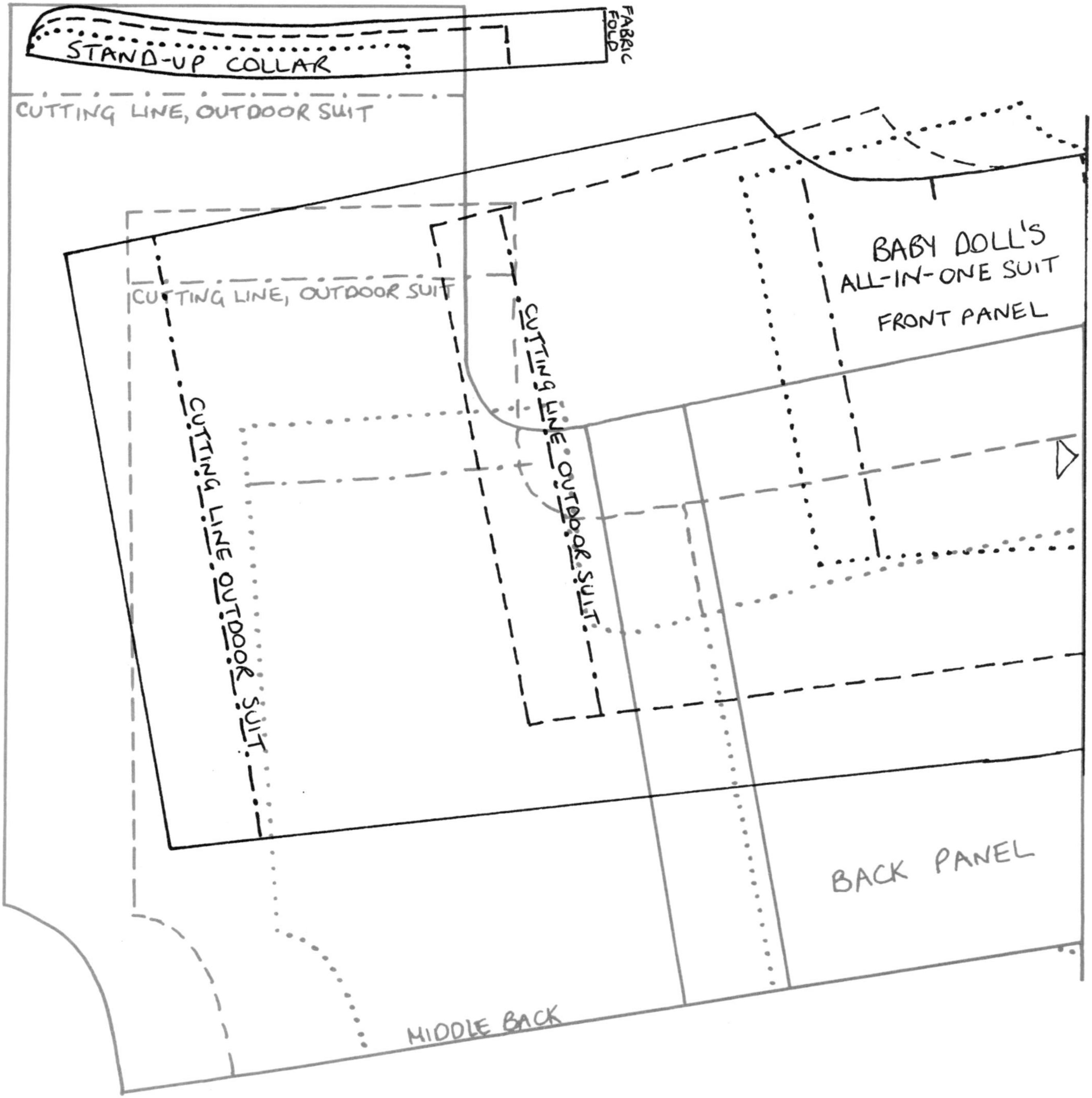

FABRIC FOLD

CUTTING LINE, OUTDOOR SUIT

CUTTING LINE, OUTDOOR SUIT

CUTTING LINE OUTDOOR SUIT

CUTTING LINE OUTDOOR SUIT

BABY DOLL'S
ALL-IN-ONE SUIT

FRONT PANEL

92

BACK PANEL

MIDDLE BACK

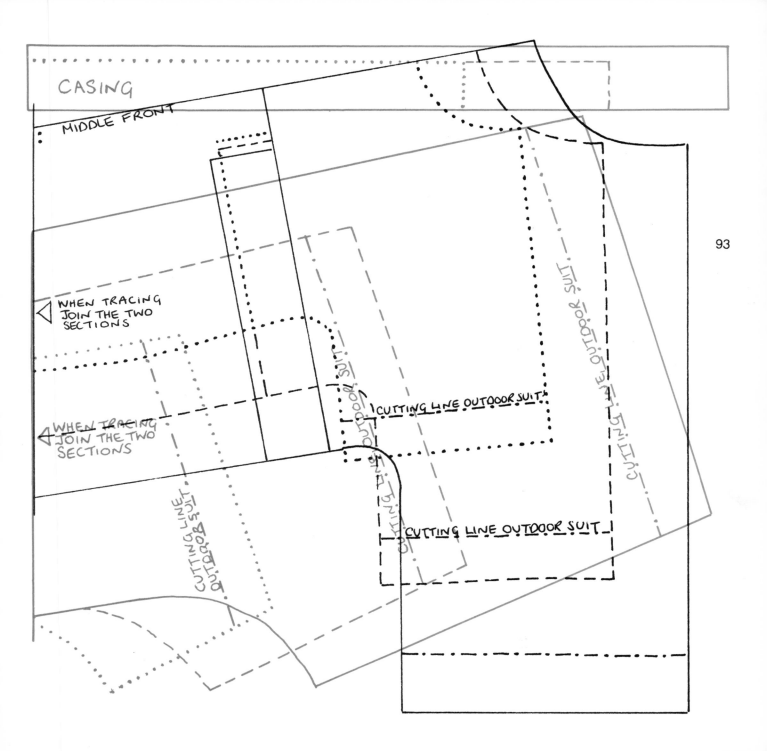

CASING

MIDDLE FRONT

WHEN TRACING
JOIN THE TWO
SECTIONS

WHEN TRACING
JOIN THE TWO
SECTIONS

CUTTING LINE OUTDOOR SUIT

CUTTING LINE OUTDOOR SUIT

CUTTING LINE OUTDOOR SUIT

CUTTING LINE OUTDOOR SUIT

CUTTING LINE OUTDOOR SUIT

93

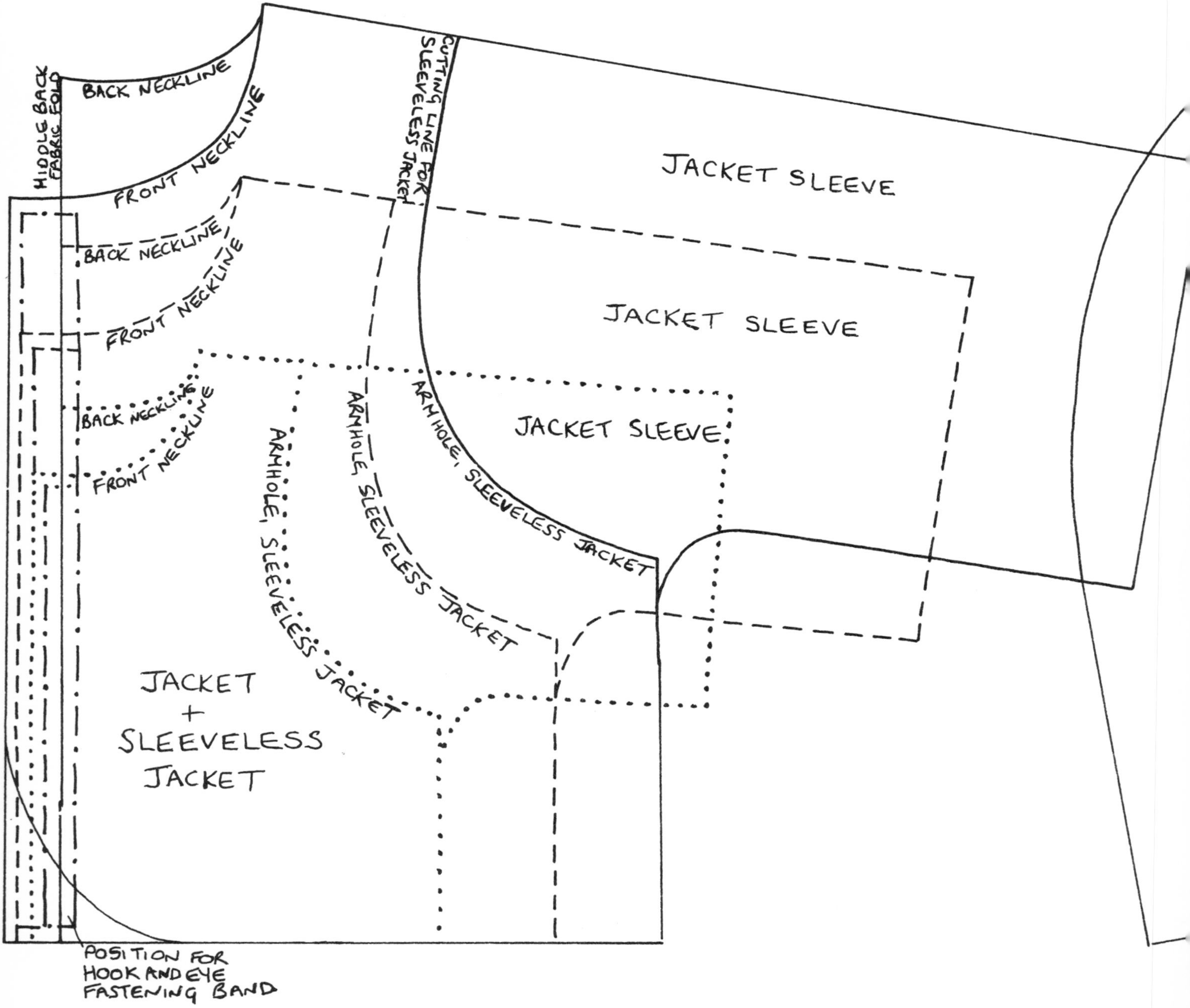

MIDDLE BACK FABRIC FOLD

BACK NECKLINE

FRONT NECKLINE

CUTTING LINE FOR SLEEVELESS JACKET

JACKET SLEEVE

BACK NECKLINE

FRONT NECKLINE

JACKET SLEEVE

BACK NECKLINE

FRONT NECKLINE

ARMHOLE, SLEEVELESS JACKET

ARMHOLE, SLEEVELESS JACKET

ARMHOLE, SLEEVELESS JACKET

JACKET SLEEVE

JACKET
+
SLEEVELESS
JACKET

POSITION FOR HOOK AND EYE FASTENING BAND

JACKET/ALL-IN-ONE SUIT
HOOD

Turtle-neck sweater

First see introduction for information about stitches used and size of needles.

Front panel
Cast on: 28, 34 or 40 stitches, according to size of doll.
Knit 4, 5, 5 rows in rib stitch.
Carry on in stocking stitch (1 row plain, 1 row purl). During the first row increase 4, 4 or 6 stitches.
Optional: knit the following rows in jacquard pattern (see introduction).
Knit to 4" (10cm), 4¾" (12cm) or 5⅛" (13cm)
Pick up the middle 8, 12 or 14 stitches on a reserve strand.
Continue knitting on both sides, and every other row pick up 1 stitch on the reserve strand. 1, 2 or 2 stitches respectively.
Continue knitting until your work measures 4½" (11.5cm), 5½" (14cm), 6¼" (16cm). Cast off the shoulder stitches or put them on a reserve strand.

Left back panel
Cast on: 16, 2; or 22 stitches, according to size of doll.
Knit 4, 5, 5 rows in rib stitch.
Continue in stocking stitch. During the first row increase 1, 2 or 3 stitches. But continue to knit the first 4 stitches on the right-hand side in rib stitch.
Optional: knit the following rows in jacquard pattern. If you decide to do so, continue to knit the first 4 stitches on the right-hand side in the main shade.
Continue to knit until your work measures 4⅛" (10.5cm), 5" (12.5cm), 5¼" (13.5cm).
Pick up 7, 8, 9 stitches from the right-hand side on a reserve strand of yarn.
Every second row pick up another 1, 2, 2 stitches on a reserve strand.
When your work measures 4½" (11.5cm), 5½" (14cm), 6¼" (16cm) pick up the shoulder stitches on a reserve strand or cast off the stitches.

Right back panel
As left back panel but in reverse.

Sleeve
Cast on: 20, 22 or 24 stitches.
Knit 3, 4, 4 rows in rib stitch.
Continue in stocking stitch.
During the first row increase 2, 4 4 stitches.

Optional: knit the following rows in jacquard pattern.
Knit until your work measures 2" (5cm), 2½" (6cm), 2¾" (7cm).
Cast off.

Construction
Baste or sew the shoulder seams together.
On the neckline pick up 36, 46, 54 stitches including the stitches from the reserve strand.
Knit in rib stitch for 1¼" (3cm), 1¾" (4.5cm), 2¼" (6cm).
Cast off.
Sew on the sleeves, having the middle of the top edge opposite the shoulder seam.
Sew the underarm side seams together.
Sew snap fasteners or hook and eye fastening band to the back.

Hooded jacket for your child   model 2

Size by age: *6-9 months, 18 mths,   3 years*
Height of child: *29" (74cm),   34" (86cm), 38" (98cm)*

Pattern pieces: front panel, back panel, hood, pocket.
Fabric needed: 54" (140cm) wide: 1¼yd (1.10m)
Lining fabric: 54" (140cm) wide: ⅜yd (0.35m)
Notions: open-ended separating zipper, 1yd (1m)
                 ruched lingerie elastic ¾" (2cm) wide

Sewing instructions:
1 Reproduce the pattern pieces on 2 x 2" (5 x 5cm) dressmaker's pattern paper. Mark the position of the pocket on the front panel.
2 With right sides together, fold the fabric in half and pin the pieces to it, having the middle of the back against the fabric fold.
3 Cut out the middle of the front with an extra ¾" (2cm) for seam allowance. The remaining edges with an extra ⅜-¾" (1-2cm) for seam allowance.
4 Cut out the hood pieces again in lining fabric.
5 Zigzag around the edges of the pieces.
6 Stitch the underarm side seams together. Clip the curve in the seam allowance and press the seams open.
7 Stitch the upper arm seams together. Press the seams open.
8 Stitch the hood sections together. Clip the curve in the seam allowance and press the seams open. Stitch the hood to the neckline.
9 Stitch the lining sections of the hood together.

10 With right sides together stitch the front edges of the hoods together. Turn the lining to the inside.
11 Clip the seam allowance of the neckline. Press the seam allowance of the hood neckline and the seam allowance of the jacket neckline up and stitch the neckline of the lining to the jacket neckline.
12 Turn in and press the seam allowance all the way around the edges of the pockets. Turn in and stitch the diagonal side at the top of the pocket and stitch the pockets on to the jacket where indicated.
13 Turn in the bottom edge of the sleeves and stitch stretched ruched lingerie elastic to the insides. (The hem of the sleeve is stitched at the same time.)

14 Turn in the bottom edge of the jacket and stitch stretched ruched lingerie elastic to the inside.
15 Stitch the zipper into the middle of the front. (See introduction for how to insert zipper.)

97

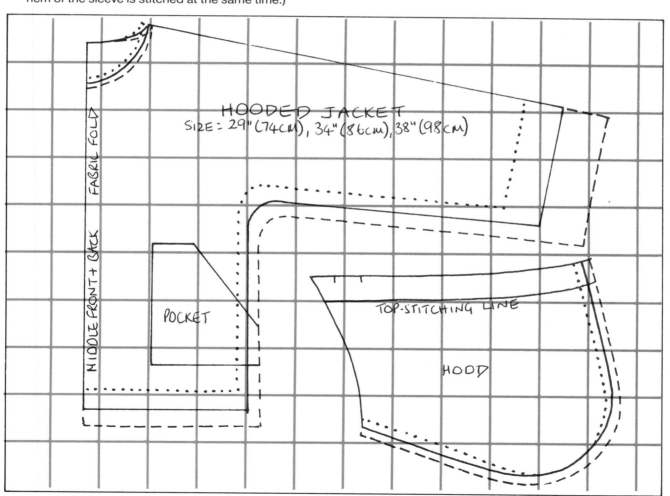

HOODED JACKET
SIZE = 29" (74CM), 34" (86CM), 38" (98CM)

FABRIC FOLD

MIDDLE FRONT + BACK

POCKET

TOP-STITCHING LINE

HOOD

Playsuit, knitted jackets, sweater and pants

Playsuit with yoke *model 1*

Pattern pieces: front yoke, back yoke, front yoke facing, back yoke facing, front panel, back panel, sleeve.
Notions: hook and eye fastening band or loops and buttons.

Sewing instructions:
1 Reproduce the pattern pieces. With right sides together, fold the fabric in half and pin the pieces to it, having the front yoke, the front yoke facing and the sleeve against the fabric fold.
2 Cut out the sleeve twice. Cut out all the pieces with an extra ⅜" (1cm) for seam allowance.
3 Zigzag around the edges of all the pieces.
4 Gather the sleeves at the upper edge.
5 Stitch the inside leg seams.
6 Stitch the crotch seam, leaving a long opening at the back.
7 Gather the front panel and the two back panels along the upper edge, until they are the same width as the front and back yoke.
8 Stitch the front panel to the front yoke.
9 Stitch the back panels to the back yokes.
10 Stitch the shoulder seams together.
11 Stitch the shoulder seams of the facings together.
12 Stitch the neckline of the front and back yoke and the neckline of the front and back facing together. Clip the seam allowance.
13 Turn in the seam allowance of the back opening and the facing and stitch along the edges.
14 Turn in the facing and top-stitch around the neckline.
15 Stitch pieces of hook and eye fastening band at the top of the opening or else attach buttons and loops.
16 Turn in the bottom edge of the sleeves and stitch stretched ruched lingerie elastic to the inside.
17 Turn in the bottom edge of the legs and stitch stretched ruched lingerie elastic to the inside.
18 Stitch the sleeves into the armholes. Clip the seam allowance.
19 Stitch the underarm side seams. Clip the curve in the seam allowance.

Pullover

First see introduction for instructions about stitches used and size of knitting·needles.

Cast on: 24, 32 or 38 stitches, according to size of doll.
Knit in plain stitch for 1¾" (4.5cm), 2½" (6.5cm), 3¼" (8.5cm).
Cast off the middle 8, 10, 12 stitches. Pick up the shoulder stitches on one side on a reserve strand of yarn.
* Carry on knitting on the other side to a length of 2½" (6.5cm), 3½" (9cm), 4¼" (11cm).
Increase 4, 5, 6 stitches on the neckline side.
Carry on knitting to a total length of 4" (10cm), 5½" (14cm), 7" (18cm).
Cast off.
Starting with the stitches from the reserve strand, repeat from * reversing instructions.

Construction
Sew a small section of the side seams together.

Knitted stretch pants *model 3, 4*

First see introduction for instructions about stitches used and size of knitting needles.

Cast on 22, 26 or 30 stitches, according to size of doll.
Knit in rib stitch: 4, 6, 8 rows.
Continue in stocking stitch. In the next row increase 16, 20, 24 stitches.
Knit to a length of 1⅜" (3.5cm), 2½" (6.5cm), 4½" (11.5cm).
Increase 1 stitch at each end of the row. This applies to all sizes.
Then, for sizes 11½" (29cm) and 14" (36cm), after 4 rows increase one stitch on each side.
For size 17" (43cm) increase 4 stitches and after 4th row increase one stitch on both sides.
Knit to 2½" (6cm), 3½" (9cm), 5⅛" (13cm).
Once you have reached this length, decrease at both ends 2 and 1, 3 and 2, 4 and 2 stitches respectively.

After 2 rows once again decrease 1 stitch at both ends. Knit to 4¾″ (12cm), 6¼″ (16cm), 8″ (20cm).

Now decrease 8, 10, 12 stitches by knitting 2 stitches together at different places in the row 8, 10 or 12 times respectively.

Now knit 3, 4, 6 rows in rib stitch.

Cast off.

Knit the other side, reversing the instructions.

Construction

Sew the pieces together.

On the inside, baste thin elastic to the top and bottom edges of the waistband. Make sure that the elastic cannot be seen on the outside.

Jacket with fabric pocket   *model 2*

First see introduction for instructions about stitches used and size of knitting needles.

Cast on:

24, 32, 38 stitches, according to size of doll. Knit in plain stitch.

Knit for ⅝″ (1.5cm), 1″ (2.5cm), 1¾″ (3.5cm). Increase 8, 12, 16 stitches on both sides.

Knit to 2¾″ (7cm), 3¼″ (8.5cm), 4″ (10cm).

Cast off the middle 8, 10, 12 stitches. Pick up the shoulder stitches on one side on a reserve strand.

Continue knitting on the other side to a length of 3½″ (9cm), 4⅛″ (10.5cm), 5″ (12.5cm).

Increase 8, 10, 12 stitches on the neckline side.

Continue knitting to a length of 5¼″ (13.5cm), 6⅛″ (15.5cm), 6⅞″ (17.5cm).

Cast off 8, 12, 16 stitches on the sleeve side.

Continue knitting to a total length of 5⅞″ (15cm), 7″ (18cm), 8¼″ (21cm).

Now pick up the stitches from the reserve strand. Knit to a length of 3½″ (9cm), 4⅛″ (10.5cm), 5″ (12.5cm). Increase 4, 4, 4 stitches on the neckline side.

Continue knitting to a length of 5¼″ (13.5cm), 6″ (15.5cm), 6⅞″ (17.5cm). Cast off 8, 12, 16 stitches on the sleeve side.

Continue knitting to a total length of 5⅞″ (15cm), 7″ (18cm), 8¼″ (21cm).

Construction

First decide which side is to wrap over on top.

Sew the underarm side seams together. Turn in and stitch along the edges of the pocket and sew this on to the jacket. Crochet loops for the buttons and sew the buttons on to the jacket.

Jacket with hood   *model 3*

First see introduction for instructions about stitches used and size of knitting needles.

Cast on: 28, 34, 40 stitches, according to size of doll.

Knit 4, 5, 5 rows in plain stitch.

Continue in stocking stitch to 1½″ (4cm), 2¼″ (5.5cm), 2½″ (6.5cm).

Increase 8, 12, 16 stitches on both sides for the sleeves.

Then knit 4, 4, 5 stitches in plain stitch at both ends and knit the stitches in between in stocking stitch.

Knit to 3½″ (9cm), 4½″ (11.5cm), 5¼″ (13.5cm).

Then, starting on one side, put 26, 36, 44 stitches on a reserve strand.

* Continue knitting with the remaining stitches. On the lower edge of the sleeve continue knitting 4, 4, 5 plain stitches and the rest in stocking stitch.

Knit 6, 8, 10 rows. After that increase 4, 7, 8 stitches on the neckline side. Now knit 4, 4, 5 plain stitches at both ends of the row and the stitches in between in stocking stitch.

Knit to a length of 6″ (15.5cm), 7⅝″ (19.5cm), 8¼″ (21.5cm).

Decrease 8, 12, 16 stitches on the sleeve side.

Carry on knitting to 7¼″ (18.5cm), 9¼″ (23.5cm), 10½″ (26.5cm).

Knit 4, 5, 5 rows in plain stitch.

Cast off.

Pick up 18, 22, 28 stitches from the side. Leave the remaining 8, 14, 16 stitches on the reserve strand.

Repeat from * but reverse the instructions.

Hood

Pick up 26, 34, 46 stitches at the neckline (including the stitches on the reserve strand).

Knit two rows, knitting the first and the last 4, 4, 5 stitches in plain stitch. Knit the remaining stitches in stocking stitch.

During the 3rd row increase 12, 14, 16 stitches. Do this in the stocking stitch.

Continue knitting to a length of 4¾″ (12cm), 6″ (15.5cm), 7½″ (19cm).

Cast off.

Instead of the hood you can knit a collar (see below).

Construction

Sew the seam along the top of the hood and sew the underarm side seam.

Make a pompom (see introduction) and sew this to the top of the hood.

Crochet loops and sew buttons to the jacket.

Collar

Pick up 26, 36, 46 stitches at the neckline (including the stitches on the reserve strand).

Knit 4, 5, 5 rows in plain stich.

Cast off.

Jacket with hood and rounded corners

Pattern pieces: front panel, back panel, hood.
Use pattern on pages 94 and 95.

Notions: remnants of wool or cotton yarn.

Sewing instructions:

1 Reproduce the pattern pieces. With right sides together, fold the fabric in half and pin the pieces to it, having the middle of the back against the fabric fold.

2 Cut out the bottom edge of the sleeve, the front of the jacket and the front of the hood without a seam allowance. The remaining edges with an extra ⅜" (1cm) for seam allowance.

3 Zigzag around the edges of all the pieces.

4 Stitch the upper arm seams.

5 Stitch the hood sections together. Clip the seam allowance.

6 Stitch the hood to the neckline. Trim the seam allowance to ¼" (0.5cm). Blanket stitch or zigzag stitch around the neckline.

7 Stitch the underarm side seams. Clip the curve in the seam allowance.

8 Blanket stitch the bottom edge of the sleeves.

9 Blanket stitch around the entire front edge of the jacket.

10 Crochet loops and attach buttons to the front opening.

Instead of blanket stitching you can crochet around the edges of the jacket, if you are using a knitted fabric.

Square-necked sweater   model 4

First see introduction for instructions about stitches used and size of knitting needles.

Front panel

Cast on: 28, 34, 40 stitches, according to size of doll.

Knit 4, 5, 5 rows in rib stitch.

Continue in stocking stitch and in the first row increase 4, 4, 5 stitches.

Optional: knit the next rows in jacquard pattern.

Knit to 4" (10cm), 4¾" (12cm), 5" (13cm).

Cast off the middle 8, 12, 14 stitches.

Carry on knitting on both sides to a length of 4½" (11.5cm), 5½" (14cm), 6" (15.5cm).

Cast off the shoulder stitches or pick them up on a reserve strand.

Left back panel

Cast on 16, 20, 22 stitches.

Knit 4, 5, 5 rows in rib stitch.

Carry on in stocking stitch but knit the first 4 stitches on the right-hand side in rib stitch. In the first row, increase 1, 2, 3 stitches.

Optional: knit the following rows in jacquard pattern. If you choose to do this, carry on knitting the first 4 stitches on the right-hand side in the main shade.

Knit to a length of 4¼" (11cm), 5" (13cm), 5¾" (14.5cm).

Cast off 7, 8, 9 stitches from the right-hand side.

Knit on from the remaining stitches until your work measures 4½" (11.5cm), 5½" (14cm), 6" (15.5cm).

Pick up the shoulder stitches on a reserve strand or cast them off.

Knit the right back panel, reversing the instructions.

Sleeve

Cast on: 20, 22, 24 stitches.

Knit 3, 4, 4 rows in rib stitch.

Carry on in stocking stitch.

In the first row increase 2, 4, 4 stitches.

Optional: knit the next rows in jacquard pattern.

Knit to a length of 2" (5cm), 2¼" (6cm), 2¾" (7cm).

Cast off.

Construction

Baste or sew the shoulder seams together. Crochet around the edge of the neckline.

Sew on the sleeves, with the middle of the upper edge against the shoulder seam.

Sew the underarm side seams together.

Sew snap fasteners or hook and eye fastening band to the back.

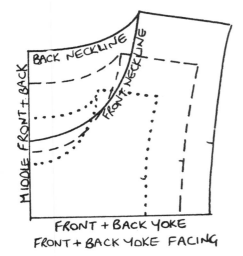

MIDDLE FRONT + BACK

BACK NECKLINE

FRONT NECKLINE

FRONT + BACK YOKE
FRONT + BACK YOKE FACING

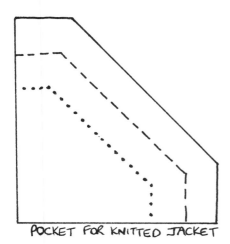

POCKET FOR KNITTED JACKET

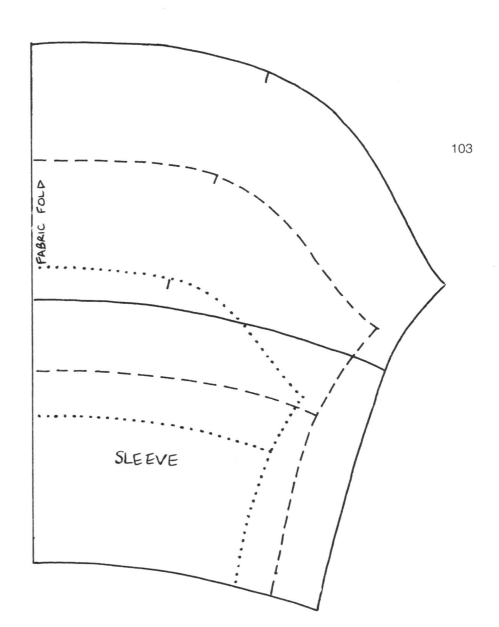

FABRIC FOLD

SLEEVE

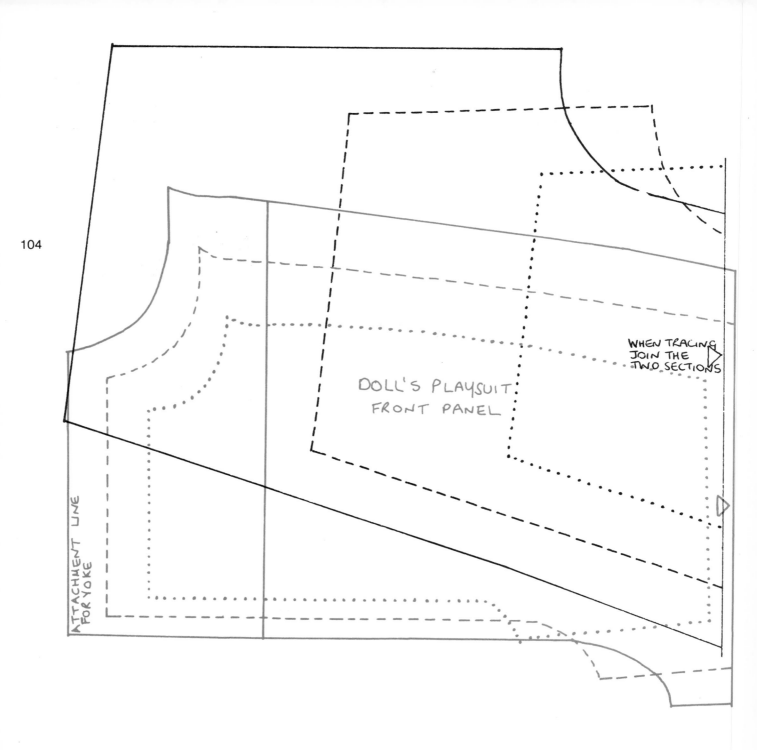

104

DOLL'S PLAYSUIT
FRONT PANEL

WHEN TRACING
JOIN THE
TWO SECTIONS

ATTACHMENT LINE
FOR YOKE

Playsuit with yoke for your child

model 1

Size by age: *0-3 mths, 3-6 mths, 9 mths-1 year*
Height of child: *24" (62cm), 27" (68cm), 29" (74cm)*
Pattern pieces: front panel, back panel, front yoke, back yoke, front yoke facing, back yoke facing, sleeve.

Fabric needed: 36" (90cm) wide: 1½yd (1.35m)
54" (140cm) wide: ¾yd (0.70m)
Notions: zipper, elastic

Sewing instructions:
1 Reproduce the pattern pieces on 2 x 2" (5 x 5cm) dressmaker's pattern paper.
2 With right sides together, fold the fabric in half and pin the pieces to it, having the front panel, front yoke, front yoke facing and the sleeve against the fold. Cut out the sleeve twice. Mark the middle of the sleeve.
3 Cut out the bottom edge of the legs and the sleeves with an extra 1" (2.5cm) for seam allowance, the middle of the back with an extra ¾" (2cm) for seam allowance. The remaining edges with an extra ⅜-¾" (1-2cm) for seam allowance.

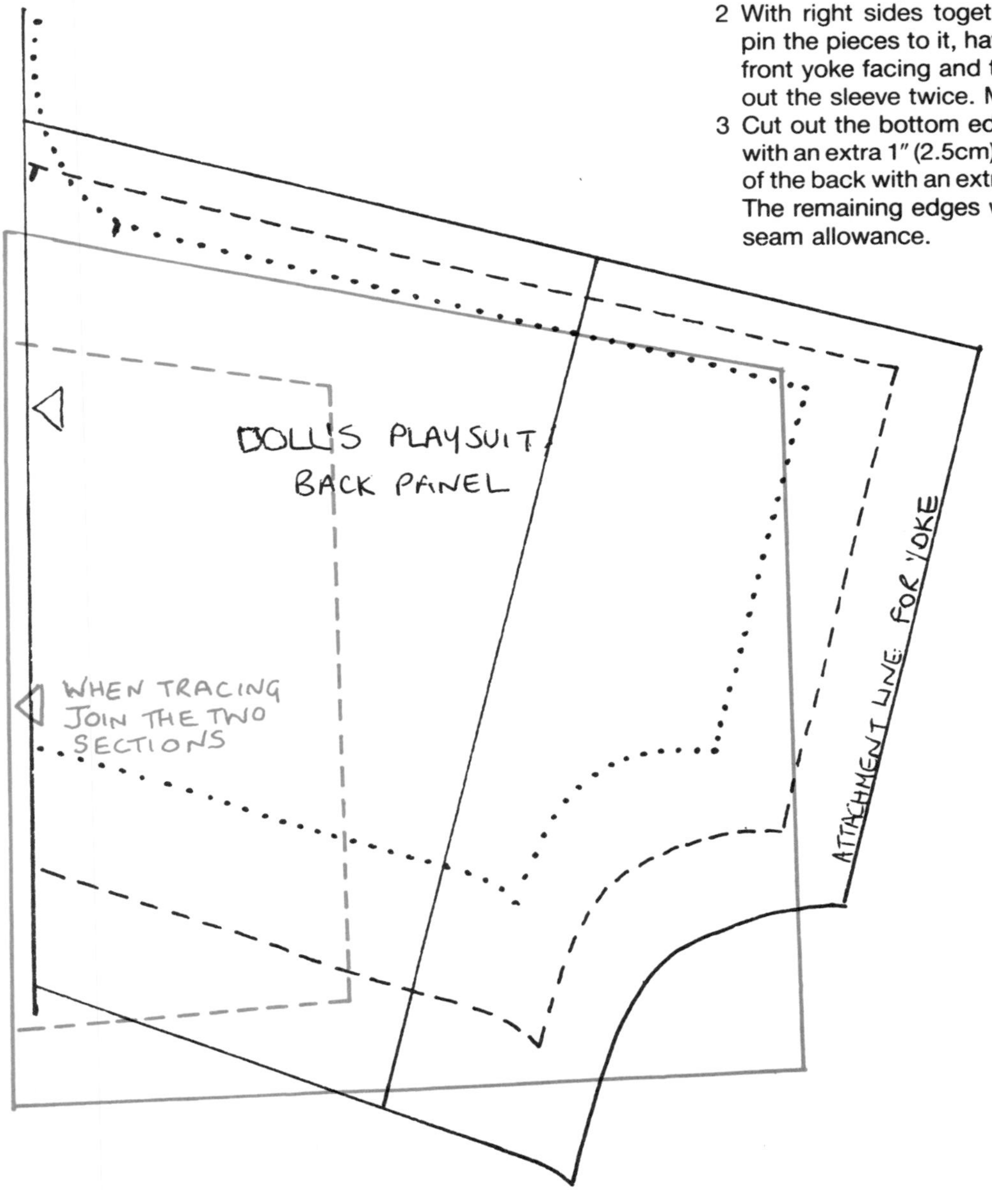

105

◁

DOLL'S PLAYSUIT
BACK PANEL

◁ WHEN TRACING
JOIN THE TWO
SECTIONS

ATTACHMENT LINE FOR YOKE

4 Zigzag around the edges of all the pieces.
5 Stitch the middle back seam together, stopping 1½″ (3.5cm) from the top.
6 Gather the front panel and stitch the front panel and front yoke together.
7 Gather the back panels and stitch these to the back yokes.
8 Stitch the zipper into the back panel. (See introduction for how to insert zipper.)
9 Stitch the crotch seam. Clip the curve in the seam allowance and press the seam open.
10 Stitch the side seams and press them open.
11 Turn in the bottom edge of the legs and stitch around them ⅝″ (1.5cm) from the edge. Leave a small opening.
12 Stitch the shoulder seams. Stitch the sleeve seams. Press them open.
13 Mark the middle of the sleeve. Place the right side of the sleeve against the right side of the armholes of the front and back panel. The shoulder seams of the front and back panel should be placed against the mark for the middle of the sleeve. Stitch together and press the seams flat.
14 Turn in 1″ (2.5cm) along the bottom edge of the sleeves and stitch ⅝″ (1.5cm) from the edge. Leave a small opening.
15 Stitch the shoulder seams of the facing together. Press the seams open.
16 With right sides together stitch the neckline of the facing and the yokes together. Clip the seam allowance and turn right side out.
17 Turn in the seam allowance on the middle back facing. Top-stitch all the way around the neckline.
18 Thread elastic through the casings, stitch the ends of elastic together and then stitch up the opening.

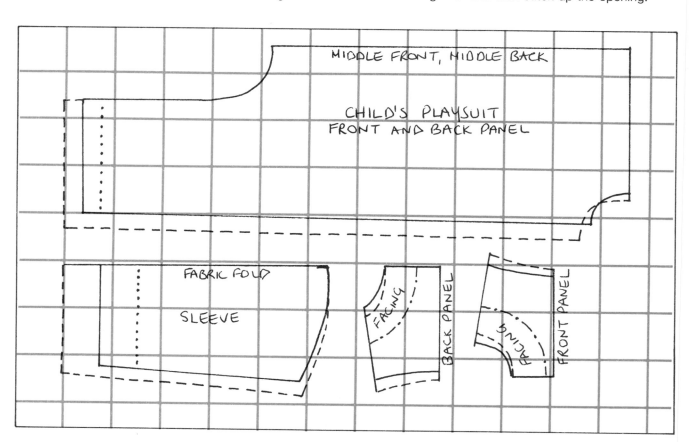

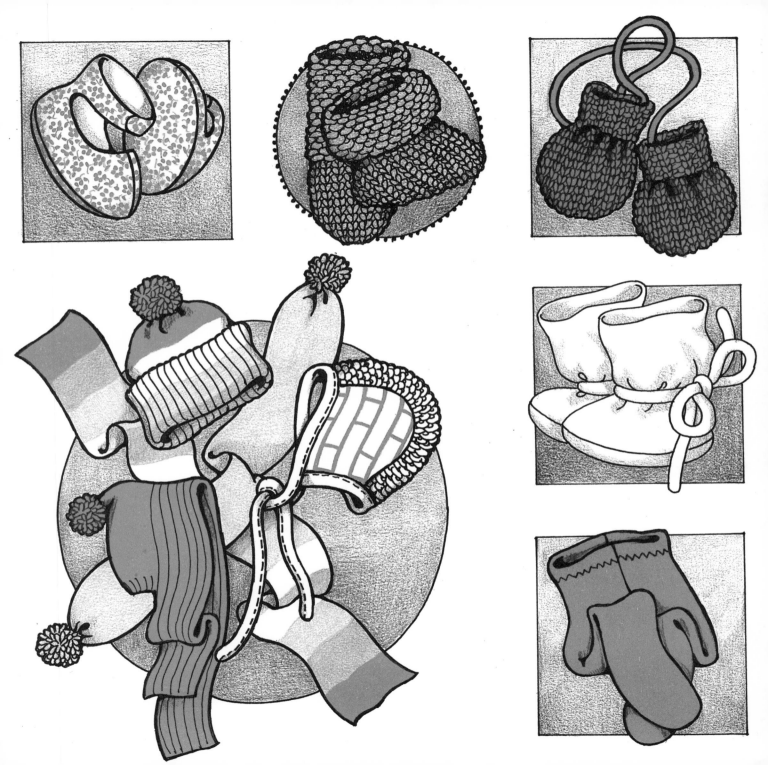

Bootees, shoes, mittens and hats

Pantyhose

Pattern pieces: front panel, back panel
Notions: elastic

Sewing instructions:
1 Reproduce the pattern, draw the highest and the lowest side of the tights. Fold the fabric in half and pin the pieces to it against the fabric fold. (You can use an old pair of tights or a thin pullover for the fabric.)
2 The front of the tights is cut low and the back is cut high. Cut out the top edge with an extra ¾" (2cm) for seam allowance. The remaining edges with an extra ¼" (0.5cm) for seam allowance.
3 Sew the inside leg seams by hand or with a zigzag stitch as far as the mark. Zigzag both edges of the seam allowance together.
4 Stitch the crotch seam by hand or using a zigzag stitch.
5 Zigzag both edges of the seam allowance together.
6 Turn in the seam allowance along the top edge and zigzag or hem it down. Leave a small opening in the middle of the back to insert the elastic.
7 Thread elastic through the casing, stitch the ends together and stitch up the opening.

Bootees

Pattern pieces: bootee, sole
Notions: cord or tape

Sewing instructions:
1 Reproduce the pattern pieces. With right sides together, fold the fabric in half and pin the pieces to it, having the back of the bootee against the fabric fold. For the fabric use imitation leather, soft leather, felt, plastic or fabric reinforced with fabric webbing.
2 Cut along the top edge without a seam allowance. The remaining edges with an extra ¼" (0.5cm) for seam allowance.
3 Zigzag around the edges of the pieces, if necessary.
4 Stitch the front of the bootee. The cord or tape (if using tape, fold it in half first) is stitched on at the same time with the folded side of the tape on the right side.
5 Stitch the sole onto the bootee.

Shoes

Pattern pieces: shoe, sole
Notions: hook and eye fastening band or snap fasteners

Sewing instructions:
1 Reproduce the pattern pieces and pin them to a double layer of imitation leather, soft leather, felt, plastic or fabric reinforced with fabric webbing.
2 Cut out the upper edge of the shoe and the ankle strap without a seam allowance. The remaining edges with an extra ¼" (0.5cm) for seam allowance.
3 Zigzag around the edges of all the pieces.
4 Stitch the back and the front seam of the foot.
5 Stitch the sole onto the foot.
6 Stitch pieces of hook and eye fastening band to the ankle strap or else sew on snap fasteners. If using leather you can cut out a buttonhole and sew on a small button.

Knitting: First see introduction for information about stitches used and size of knitting needles.

Mittens

Cast on 12, 14 or 16 stitches, according to size of doll.
Knit ⅜" (1cm), ½" (1.25cm), ⅝" (1.5cm) in rib stitch.
Continue in stocking stitch.
Increase 2, 4, 6 stitches on the first row.
Knit to 1½" (4cm), 2" (5cm), 2¼" (6cm).
For the next 2 rows keep knitting 2 stitches together.
Cast off.
Sew up the seams.
Crochet or buy a cord to join the mittens. Sew the mittens to the cord.

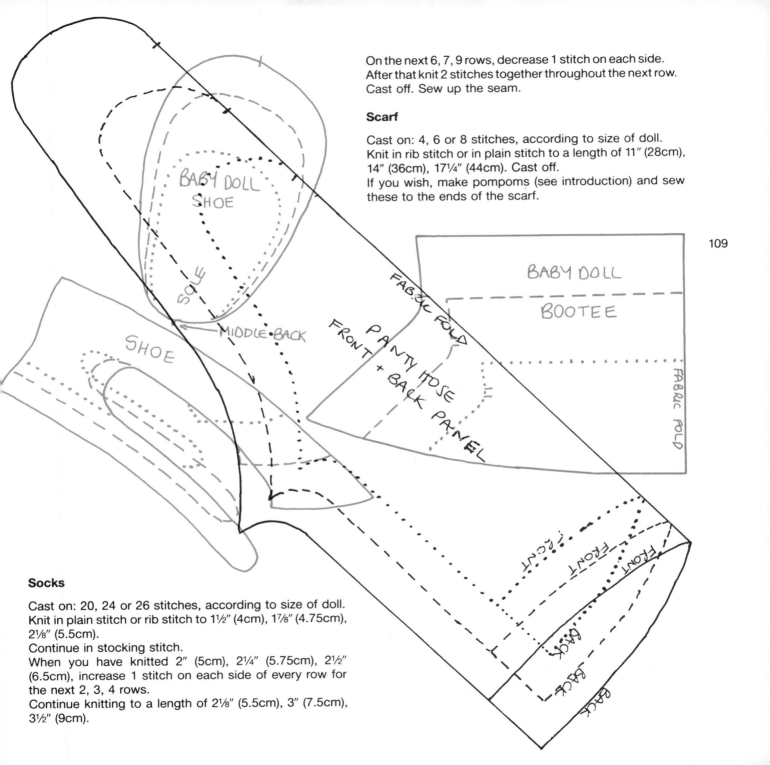

On the next 6, 7, 9 rows, decrease 1 stitch on each side.
After that knit 2 stitches together throughout the next row.
Cast off. Sew up the seam.

Scarf

Cast on: 4, 6 or 8 stitches, according to size of doll.
Knit in rib stitch or in plain stitch to a length of 11″ (28cm),
14″ (36cm), 17¼″ (44cm). Cast off.
If you wish, make pompoms (see introduction) and sew
these to the ends of the scarf.

109

BABY DOLL
SHOE

SOLE

MIDDLE·BACK

SHOE

FABRIC FOLD

PANTY HOSE
FRONT + BACK PANEL

BABY DOLL
BOOTEE

FABRIC FOLD

FRONT

FRONT

FRONT

BACK

BACK

BACK

Socks

Cast on: 20, 24 or 26 stitches, according to size of doll.
Knit in plain stitch or rib stitch to 1½″ (4cm), 1⅞″ (4.75cm),
2⅛″ (5.5cm).
Continue in stocking stitch.
When you have knitted 2″ (5cm), 2¼″ (5.75cm), 2½″
(6.5cm), increase 1 stitch on each side of every row for
the next 2, 3, 4 rows.
Continue knitting to a length of 2⅛″ (5.5cm), 3″ (7.5cm),
3½″ (9cm).

Hat with pompom

Cast on: 40, 50 or 60 stitches, according to size of doll.
Knit in rib stitch to a length of 2" (5cm), 2¼" (6cm), 2¾" (7cm).
Continue in stocking stitch to a length of 4" (10cm), 4¾" (12cm), 5½" (14cm).
Throughout the next two rows knit 2 stitches together.
Cast off the remaining stitches.
Sew up the seam and then thread a strand of yarn through the stitches at the top of the hat. Pull this tight and sew it down.
Make a pompom (see introduction) and sew this to the top.

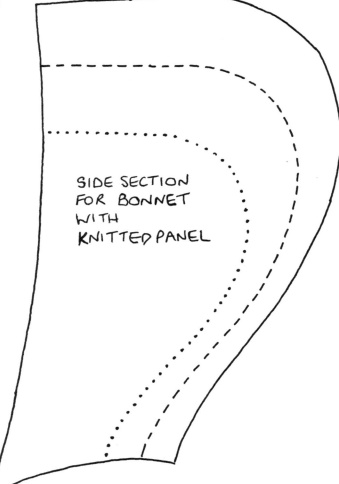

SIDE SECTION FOR BONNET WITH KNITTED PANEL

Bonnet with knitted panel

Pattern pieces: ear piece
Notions: bias binding (if a cord is crocheted the bias binding can be omitted)

Sewing instructions:
1 Knit in plain stitch a panel measuring 2⅜ x 5¾" (6 x 14.5cm), 3 x 7" (7.5 x 17.5cm) or 3 x 8" (9 x 20.5cm).
2 Reproduce the pattern.
3 With right sides together, fold the fabric in half and pin the pattern to it. Cut out with an extra ⅜" (1cm) for seam allowance all the way around.
4 Turn in and stitch the seam allowance on the front edge.
5 Using a zigzag stitch, stitch the knitted panel to the upper edge of the ear pieces. Clip the seam allowance and turn the bonnet right side out.
6 Crochet a border around the edge of the bonnet. Crochet cords to make a tie fastening or sew bias binding around the bottom edge and then around the front edge. Leave enough tape hanging out on both sides to tie in a bow.

Hooded scarf

Cast on 4, 4 or 6 stitches and knit for 5½" (14cm), 6¾" (17cm), 8" (20cm).
Repeat on another pair of needles for the second scarf.
On the second scarf, using the same knitting needles, cast on an additional 26 stitches.
Now pick up the stitches from the first scarf and join the two scarves by knitting 4, 4, 6 rows in rib stitch. The scarves are now at opposite ends of the knitting.
Continue knitting the first and last 4, 4, 6 stitches in rib stitch. Knit the stitches in between in stocking stitch.
Increase 8, 10, 12 stitches in the stocking stitches.
Knit to a length of 4¾" (12cm), 5¾" (14.5cm), 6¾" (17cm). Cast off.
With the right sides together, match up the front edges and sew up the seam on top of the hood.
Make a pompom (see introduction) and sew this to the top.

Backpack and baby carrier

Baby carrier

Pattern pieces: middle section, side band, top strap, bottom strap.
Notions: 3¼yd (3m) twill band 1½" (4cm) wide, elastic, 2 D-rings 1¼" (3cm) long.

Sewing instructions:
1 Reproduce the pattern pieces. With right sides together, fold the fabric in half and pin the pieces to it, having the middle section and the side section against the fabric fold.
2 Cut out both pieces twice with an extra ⅜" (1cm) for seam allowance. Cut out two straps in twill band. Cut one band 13¾" (35cm) long and one band 2¾yds (2.50m) long.
3 Zigzag around the edges of the pieces.
4 Stitch the middle section and the middle section facing to the leg hole facings. Clip the seam allowance and turn the right side out. Top-stitch around the leg holes.
5 Iron in the seam allowances on both side sections and press the side bands in half lengthwise. Stitch them to the sides of the middle section. Thread pieces of elastic measuring 3¼" (8cm), 4¼" (11cm), 6¼" (16cm) respectively through both side sections. Sew down the elastic at the top and bottom.
6 Fold the 13¾" (35cm) twill band lengthwise and stitch it along the bottom edge of the baby carrier. Place the middle of the band on the middle of the middle section.
7 Fold the 2¾yds (2.50m) twill band lengthwise and stitch it around the top edge of the baby carrier. Place the middle of the band on the middle of the middle section.
8 Stitch the D-rings to the ends of the lower strap.

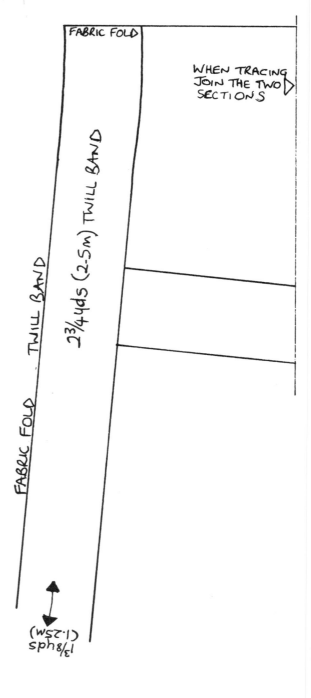

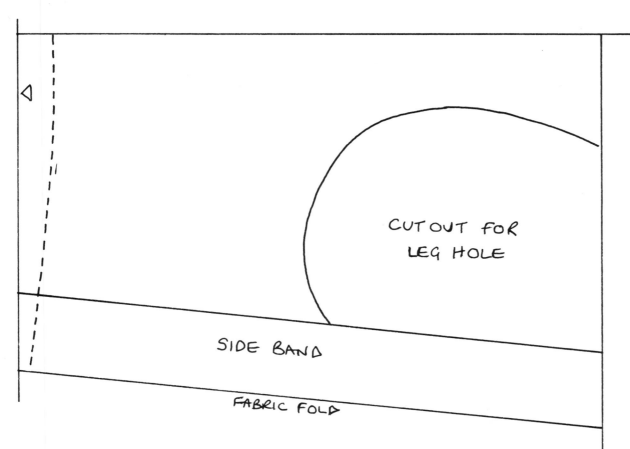

CUTOUT FOR
LEG HOLE

SIDE BAND

FABRIC FOLD

TWILL BAND 1½" (4CM) WIDE

FABRIC FOLD

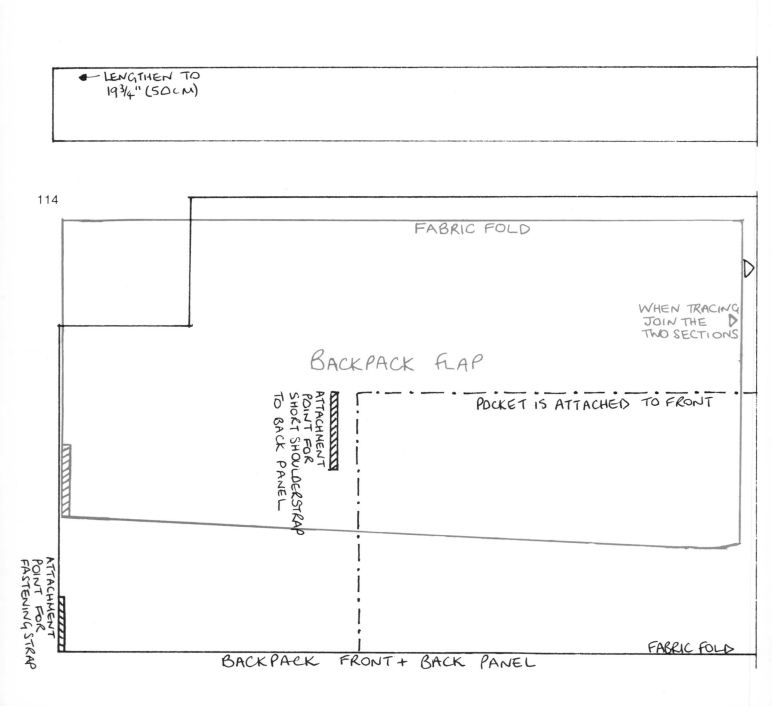

LENGTHEN TO
19¾" (50 CM)

114

FABRIC FOLD

WHEN TRACING
JOIN THE
TWO SECTIONS

BACKPACK FLAP

ATTACHMENT POINT FOR SHORT SHOULDERSTRAP TO BACK PANEL

POCKET IS ATTACHED TO FRONT

ATTACHMENT POINT FOR FASTENING STRAP

FABRIC FOLD

BACKPACK FRONT + BACK PANEL

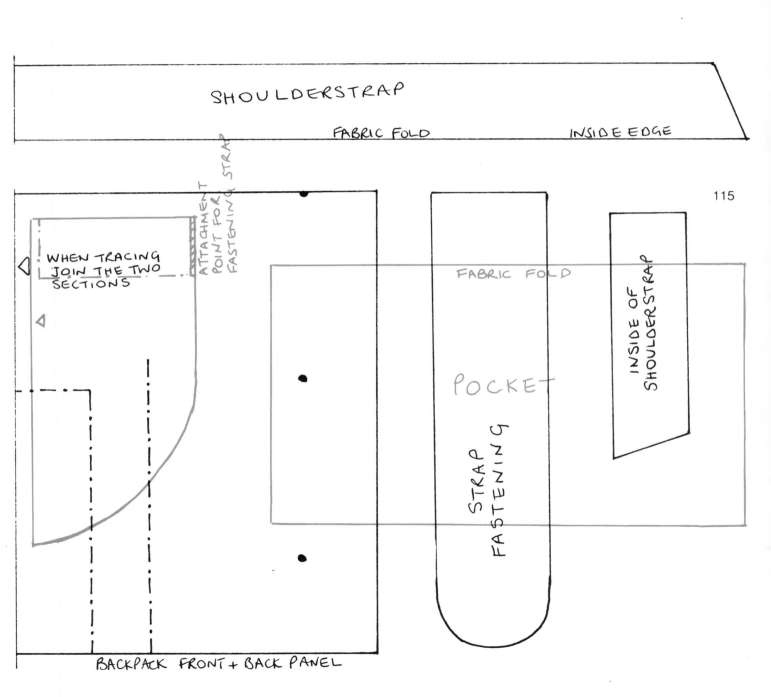

SHOULDERSTRAP

FABRIC FOLD   INSIDE EDGE

ATTACHMENT POINT FOR FASTENING STRAP

WHEN TRACING JOIN THE TWO SECTIONS

FABRIC FOLD

INSIDE OF SHOULDERSTRAP

POCKET

STRAP FASTENING

BACKPACK FRONT + BACK PANEL

115

Child's backpack

Pattern pieces: front panel backpack, back panel back-pack, pocket, flap, fastening strap, bottom section shoulder strap, top section shoulder strap.

Notions: rings, 4 D-rings, cord, hook and eye fastening band or a snap fastener.

Sewing instructions:

1 Reproduce the pattern pieces. Lengthen the shoulder strap to measure 19¾" (50cm). Mark the positions of the flap, the shoulder straps, the rings, the fastening straps and the pocket.

2 With right sides together, fold the fabric in half and pin the pieces to it, having all the pieces except the fastening strap against the fabric fold. Cut out with an extra ⅜" (1cm) for seam allowance. Cut out the flap, the shoulder straps and the fastening strap twice. If you wish to finish the edge of the flap with binding, there is no need to cut a seam allowance on the outer edge of the flap.

3 Zigzag around the edges of all the pieces.

4 Stitch the corner seams of the front and back panel.

5 Stitch the pocket to the front panel.

6 Stitch the flap pieces together, clip the seam allowance and turn right side out. Top-stitch all the way around or stitch bias binding around the outer edge. Turn in the seam allowance on the bottom edge of the flap and stitch the bottom edge together.

7 Fold the shoulder straps in half lengthwise and stitch them.

8 Stitch the diagonal side of the lower section of the shoulder straps to the back panel. Stitch two D-rings onto the lower sections of the shoulder straps. Take care to sew on the shoulder straps so that they slant out.

9 Stitch the flap to the back panel. At the same time sew on the shoulder straps where indicated. Take care that the shoulder straps are slanting out.

10 Fold the fastening straps in half lengthwise and stitch them. Clip the seam allowance and turn them right side out. Top-stitch all the way around them.

11 Stitch a fastening strap to the top of the flap.

12 Stitch the front and the back panel of the backpack together all the way around. Don't forget to sew on the strap fastening to the lower section at the same time.

13 Turn in and stitch the seam allowance around the top edge of the backpack.

14 Sew pieces of hook and eye fastening band to the strap fastenings or attach a snap fastener.

15 Sew rings on to the upper section of the backpack where indicated. Thread a cord through the rings.

Portable crib, hot-water bottle cover, toilet-bag, patchwork quilt

Portable crib

Pattern pieces: crib, handle
Notions: piece of strong cardboard measuring 9 x 17″ (23.5 x 43.5cm)
optional: foam rubber ⅜″ (1cm) thick for the sides, 2 pieces measuring 6 x 10″ (15 x 25cm) and 2 pieces measuring 6 x 18″ (15 x 45cm).

Sewing instructions:
1 Reproduce the pattern pieces on 2 x 2″ (5 x 5cm) dressmaker's pattern paper.
2 Fold the fabric in half and pin the pattern pieces to it. Cut out with an extra ⅝″ (1.5cm) for seam allowance. Mark the positions of the stitching lines.
3 Zigzag around the edges of the pieces.
4 With the right sides on the outside, place the crib pieces on top of each other. To hold in the cardboard stitch the seam lines together on the two longest sides and one of the short sides. Insert the cardboard. Then stitch the last seam together.
5 Stitch the handles together. Sew them where indicated on the right side of the fabric, having the closed edge on top.
6 Clip the corners as far as the cardboard seam lines. Now stitch together the seams to form the corners. Hand stitch the two flaps on the corner seams together stopping ¾″ (2cm) from the top edge.
7 Now turn the right side out. Optional: insert foam rubber into the side panels, turn in the seam allowance along the top edge and stitch all the way around.

Hot-water bottle cover

Pattern pieces: side, base
Notions: bias binding

Sewing instructions:
1 Reproduce the pattern pieces. With right sides together, fold the fabric in half and pin the side piece to it against the fabric fold. Cut out the base on single fabric.
2 Cut out with an extra ⅜″ (1cm) for seam allowance.
3 Zigzag around the edges of all the pieces.
4 Turn in and stitch the seam allowance along the top edge. Stitch the side seam. Fold a length of bias binding in half lengthwise and stitch along it or else use a length of cord and stitch it on to the upper edge where indicated. Be sure that the ends are hanging out on the right side.
5 Stitch on the bottom section. Clip the seam allowance and turn the right side out.

Toilet-bag

Notions: 4″ (10cm) zipper

Sewing instructions:
1 Reproduce the square. Cut it out in fabric twelve times with an extra ⅜″ (1cm) for seam allowance. Zigzag around the edges of all the pieces.
2 Stitch 6 squares together – three squares on top and three underneath. Do this twice.
3 Now you have two pieces of fabric. Stitch the zipper (see introduction) in between these two pieces of fabric on the long side. Leave the tab hanging out. This will hang free inside the bag.
4 Stitch all the way around the bag. Clip the corners of the seam allowance. Turn the bag right side out.

Patchwork quilt

Make this by cutting out 45 squares measuring 2 x 2″ (5 x 5cm) twice; allow ⅜″ (1cm) for seam allowance. Zigzag around the edges of the squares and stitch them together to form two pieces of fabric 10 x 18″ (25 x 45cm).
With right sides together stitch these two pieces of fabric together on three sides. Clip the corners and turn the right side out. Fill the quilt with lining material and sew up the open side. Distribute the filling evenly and stitch along the seamlines of the patchwork squares.

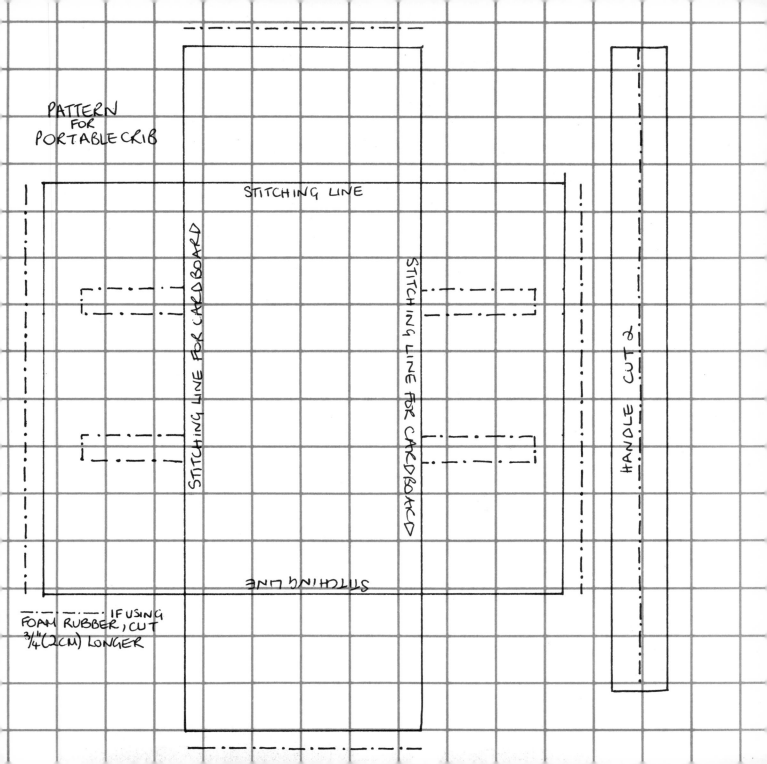

PATTERN
FOR
PORTABLE CRIB

STITCHING LINE

STITCHING LINE FOR CARDBOARD

STITCHING LINE FOR CARDBOARD

STITCHING LINE

HANDLE CUT 2

IF USING
FOAM RUBBER, CUT
¾" (2 CM) LONGER

Mattress: make a cover for a piece of foam rubber measuring 9½ x 17¼" (24 x 44cm) and ¾" (2cm) thick.

Sheet: stitch a piece of fabric measuring 13¾ x 21½" (35 x 55cm).

Rubber sheet: cut a piece of polythene 8 x 12" (20 x 30cm).

Flannelette undersheet: cut a piece of flannelette measuring 17¾ x 10" (45 x 25cm). Blanket stitch around the edges.

Pillow: use a piece of fabric measuring 7 x 4" (18 x 10cm) and stitch the seams together on three sides. Turn right side out. Stuff with filling, turn in the seam allowances on the open side and stitch together.

Pillowcase: use a piece of fabric 18 x 4¼" (46 x 11cm). Cut out with an extra ⅝" (1.5cm) for seam allowance. Zigzag around the edges. Turn in and stitch the seam allowances on the short ends. Turn in 3" (8cm) on one side and 7½" (19cm) on the other side. With right sides together stitch the two long edges together. Turn the pillow case right side out.

120

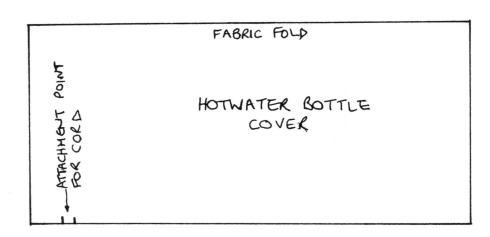

Doll's crib, table and chair

Bed furnishings

Mattress

Make a cover for a piece of foam rubber 1½" (4cm) thick. The foam rubber should be the same size as the sheet of cardboard, but if you prefer you can have the foam rubber slightly smaller. Cut off the corners.

Rubber sheet: piece of polythene 11¾ x 15¾" (30 x 40cm).

Flannelette undersheet: piece of flannelette 17¾ x 23½" (45 x 60cm). Blanket stitch around the edges.

Pillow: use a length of fabric measuring 11¾ x 8" (30 x 20cm) and stitch the seams together on three sides. Stuff with filling. Turn in the seam allowance on the open side and stitch the seam together.

Pillowcase: a length of fabric 28¼ x 8" (72 x 20cm).
Cut out with an extra ⅝" (1.5cm) for seam allowance. Zigzag around the edges. Turn in and stitch the seam allowances at both ends. On one side turn in 4¾" (12cm) and on the other side turn in 11¾" (30cm). Stitch the two side seams together. Turn the pillowcase right side out.

Patchwork quilt

Cut out 48 squares each measuring 4 x 4" (10 x 10cm); allow an extra ⅜" (1cm) for seam allowance. Zigzag around the edges of the squares and then sew them together to make two pieces measuring 15¾ x 23½" (40 x 60cm). With right sides together stitch the two pieces together on three sides. Clip the corners and turn the right side out. Stuff the quilt with filling and stitch the open side together. Distribute the filling evenly and then stitch along the seamlines of the squares.

Canopy

Use a piece of fabric measuring 1⅝yds x 36" (1.5m x 90cm) and a rod. Turn in and stitch the edges of the fabric on three sides. Leave the bottom edge measuring 1⅝yds (1.5m). Gather the stitched long edge until it measures twice the length of the upper edge of the rod.
Gather the fabric again 1½" (4cm) underneath so that it measures twice the length of the upper edge of the rod.
With the right sides on the outside, fold the gathered piece of fabric in half.
Stitch the top edge together and then stitch once again 1½" (4cm) below this.
Sew the front edge together between the gathered sections.
Push the canopy over the rod.
Measure the length you want the canopy and then turn in the bottom edge and stitch it.

Before buying wood, look around to see if you can find wood remnants. These are often obtainable from a carpenter. In this way you can make an attractive bed or chair for very little money.

Crib

Material:

4 bars	1½ x 1½" (4 x 4cm), 18" (46cm) long
4 bars	1 x 1" (2.5 x 2.5cm), 14" (60cm) long
4 bars	1 x 1" (2.5 x 2.5cm), 13¾" (35cm) long

Ask a carpenter to make a groove lengthwise in the bars. The groove should be the same width as the thickness of the plywood.

10 round bars ½" (14mm) diameter, 15¾" (40cm) long [flat drill bit ½" (14mm)]

For the head and foot ends:
2 sheets of plywood ±⅜" (1cm) thick, 12¼ x 13¾" (31 x 35cm)
plywood

For the base:
2 plywood bars ⅜ x ⅜" (1 x 1cm), 24" (60cm) long
2 plywood slats ⅜ x ⅜" (1 x 1cm), 13¾" (35cm) long
1 sheet plywood 14½ x 24½" (37 x 62cm)
12 wood plugs 1¾" (44mm) diameter
8 screws 2¼" (6cm) long
small screws about ⅝" (1.5cm) long

metal rod for the canopy ± 43¼" (1.10m)
2 clamps for the rod
wood glue

Carpentry instructions:
Place the four 24" (60cm) 1 x 1" (2.5 x 2.5cm) bars side by side. Using a set square, draw a line to mark every 4" (10cm). Mark the middle of each line. Do this on all four bars.
Now drill holes ⅝" (1.5cm) deep. Use a drill stand or support while doing this.
Now try the round bars into the holes. If the bars are a little too thick, you can sandpaper around the ends of them. Sandpaper or plane the corners of the rectangular bars to smooth them off.

Now take a rectangular bar with the holes on top. Spread a little glue in each hole and fit the round bars into the holes. Spread some glue into the holes in another bar and put this on top of the round bars. Push the bars into the holes. Wipe off the excess glue immediately.
Now measure the round bars to make sure that they are all 12" (30cm) long. If necessary, use a wooden hammer to knock the bars further into the holes. Protect the wood while doing this so that it is not damaged.
Repeat this with the other two rectangular bars and the round bars.

Place the four 18" (46cm) 1½ x 1½" (4 x 4cm) bars side by side. Measure 2" (5cm) from the ends and make a mark. Starting at the 2" (5cm) marks measure a further 1" (2.5cm) at each end. Mark the middle of the bars by drawing a cross (see diagram 1).

Draw a line lengthwise along the middle of the bars. On this line mark the middle of the width of the bars.
Now using a ¼" (4mm) drill, make holes at the three marks. The holes should be half the length of the wood plugs. Do this on all four of the bars.
Sandpaper the bars.

Now take the four bars with the groove. Put some glue into the grooves. Don't use too much glue. Glue the bars to the top and the bottom end of the plywood (if necessary hammer a small nail in at the ends). Remove excess glue immediately.
Decide on the positions in which the wood plugs are to be attached (see diagram 2).
Now using a ¼" (4mm) drill make holes in the three indi-cated positions; the holes should be half the length of the wood plugs. Do this on all four sides.
Put some glue into the holes in the head end and the foot end and put the plugs into the holes.
Put some glue on to the flat parts on the side of the plywood sheets and press the sides against the 1½ x 1½" (4 x 4cm) rectangular bars. The wood plugs are thus pushed into the drilled holes.

Now drill a hole in the 1½ x 1½" (4 x 4cm) bed posts, on the side facing the sides of the bed. The hole should be drilled right through the middle of the post, 2½" (6.25cm) from the end of the post at both ends. First check the diameter of the wood screws (see diagram 3). Screw the sides to the head end and the foot end.

Now choose which side you want to have as the bottom of the bed. Screw and glue on the plywood slats at the same level as the base of the 1 x 1" (2.5 x 2.5cm) bars. (Pre-drill the slats). Check the measurements of the base of the bed. Cut the corners off the sheet of plywood. Place this in the bed and, if you wish, screw down.

Finishing:
Sandpaper the whole bed, lacquer, sandpaper again and lacquer once or twice more. You can also paint or varnish it.
If you wish you can buy protective caps for the screws.
To support the canopy: bend over the top end of the metal rod. Fix the rod to the head end with clamps.

Doll's table

Material:

4 wooden bars	¾ x ¾" (2 x 2cm), 16" (40cm) long
6 wooden bars	¾ x ¾" (2 x 2cm), 12" (30cm) long
Plywood	12 x 12 x ⅝" (30 x 30 x 1.5cm) with plastic surface if preferred
	13½ x 12 x ⅝" (34 x 30 x 1.5cm) with plastic surface if preferred
Wood plugs	12 measuring ¼" (4mm)
	Screws measuring 1⅜" (3.5cm) long

Carpentry instructions:

* Place the four long bars side by side. Starting at each end measure ¾" (2cm) in. Draw lines on the bars and mark the middle of the measured ends (see diagram 4).
Measure 6¾" (17cm) from the ends of the bars and then ¾" (2cm) (the thickness of the wood).
Draw crosses to find the middle (see diagram 4).
Drill holes ¼" (4mm) in diameter, about ⅜" (1cm) deep.
Take the remaining 6 bars. At the top of each bar draw a cross to mark the middle. Drill the depth of the wood plug – ⅜" (1cm).
Put some glue into the holes and insert the wood plugs.
Put some glue into the drilled holes on the long bars and attach three short bars to two long bars. Repeat this step.
Now you have the sides of the table.
Sandpaper the sides and, if necessary, round off the corners.*
Now attach the 13½ x 12" (34 x 30cm) plywood sheet to the two long bars.
Use the screws to do this.
Now attach the 12 x 12" (30 x 30cm) plywood to the middle bars. The side should touch the previous sheet of plywood.
Use the screws to attach the plywood. The chair will be on this side of the table.

Finishing: lacquer the table, sandpaper and lacquer twice more.

CRIB AND CHAIR
(DIAGRAMS 1–4)

2

1

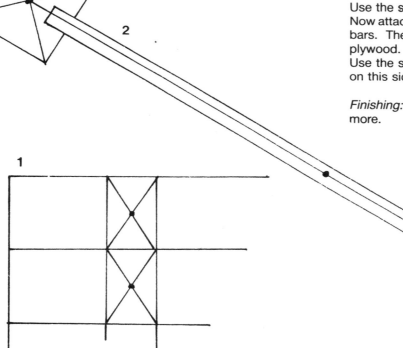

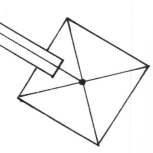

Chair

Material:

	10 wooden bars ¾ x ¾" (2 x 2cm) 10" (25cm) long
Plywood:	10 x 10 x ⅝" (25 x 25 x 1.5cm)
	10¼ x 10 x ⅝" (26 x 25 x 1.5cm)
	4¾ x 11½ x ⅝" (12 x 29 x 1.5cm)

All above with plastic surface if preferred
12 wood plugs measuring ¼" (4mm)
8 screws measuring 1½" (3.5cm)
optional: 2 flat-headed bolts (±1½" (4cm) with protective cap.

Carpentry instructions:

For the underneath of the chair follow the instructions for the table from * to *.

The in-between bar is now placed exactly in the middle.

Now attach the 10 x 10" (25 x 25cm) plywood sheet between the middle bars.

Use the screws to do this. This is the seat.

Now attach the 10¼ x 10" (26 x 25cm) plywood between the armrests. See that the underneath of the plywood is on the same level as the underneath of the seat. If you wish round off the corners on the upper edge.

Attach the 4¾ x 11½" (12 x 29cm) plywood on to the front of the armrests, so it sticks out ⅝" (1.5cm) at the front.

125

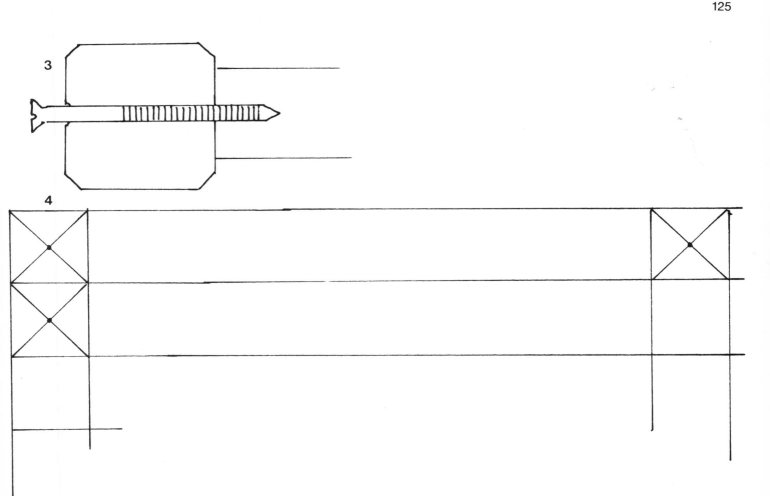

Stand-up Dolls

Clothes for a stand-up doll

T-shirt *model 1*

Pattern pieces: front panel, back panel
Fabric needed: tricot/knitted fabric
Notions: hook and eye fastening band

Sewing instructions:
1 Reproduce the pattern pieces. With right sides together, fold the fabric in half and pin the pieces to it, having the middle of the front against the fabric fold.
2 Cut out with an extra ⅜″ (1cm) for seam allowance.
3 Zigzag around the edges of the pieces.
4 Stitch the shoulder seams and the side seams with a gentle zigzag stitch.
5 Turn in the seam allowance all the way around.
6 Stitch hook and eye fastening band to the back.

Panties

For pattern and instructions use baby dolls, model 5, p58.
Fabric needed: tricot/knitted fabric

Nightdress model 2

Pattern pieces: front panel, back panel, front neckline facing, back neckline facing.
Notions: hook and eye fastening band or buttons and loops, ruched lingerie elastic

Sewing instructions:
1 Reproduce the pattern pieces on 2 x 2″ (5 x 5cm) dressmaker's pattern paper. With right sides together, fold the fabric in half and pin the pieces to it, having the middle of the front and the front neckline facing against the fold. Mark the stitching lines for the pleats.
2 Cut out with an extra ⅜″ (1cm) for seam allowance.
3 Zigzag around the edges of the pieces.
4 Stitch the pleats in the front and the back panel.
5 Stitch the front neckline facing to the neckline. Clip the seam allowance.
6 Stitch the back neckline facings to the neckline. Clip the seam allowance.
7 Stitch the upper arm seams on the facing and the front and back panel together at the same time. Turn the facing right side out and top-stitch around the neckline.
8 Turn in the seam allowance at the end of the sleeves and stitch stretched ruched lingerie elastic to the inside of the ends of the sleeves. In this way the bottom edge of the sleeve is finished at the same time.
9 Stitch the underarm side seams. Clip the curve in the seam allowance.
10 Turn in and stitch the bottom edge.
11 Turn in and stitch both back sections. Stitch pieces of hook and eye fastening band to the top of the back opening or sew on buttons and loops.

Nightclothes model 3

Pattern pieces
(top): front panel, back panel
Notions: hook and eye fastening band, knitted cuffs for the sleeves and bottom edge.

Sewing instructions:
1 Reproduce the pattern pieces. With right sides together, fold the fabric in half and pin the pieces to it, having the middle of the front against the fabric fold.
2 Cut out with an extra ⅜″ (1cm) for seam allowance.
3 Zigzag around the edges of the pieces.
4 Stitch the upper arm seams.
5 Stitch knitted cuffs to the ends of the sleeves.
6 Stitch the underarm side seams together. Clip the curve in the seam allowance.
7 Turn in and stitch the seam allowance on the back sections.
8 Stitch the collar to the neckline.
9 Stitch the knitted cuff to the bottom edge.
10 Stitch pieces of hook and eye fastening band to the back.

Pattern pieces

(pants):	pants front, pants back
Notions:	2 knitted cuffs, elastic

Sewing instructions:

1 Reproduce the pattern pieces on 2 x 2" (5 x 5cm) dressmaker's pattern paper. Fold the fabric in half and pin the pieces to it.
2 Cut out the top edge with an extra ¾" (2cm) for seam allowance. The remaining edges with an extra ⅜" (1cm) for seam allowance.
3 Zigzag around the eges of the pieces.
4 Stitch the inside leg seams of the front and the back together with a gentle zigzag stitch.
5 Stitch the front panel crotch seam together. Repeat with the back panels. Clip the curve in the seam allowance.
6 Stitch knitted cuffs to the ends of the legs.
7 Stitch the side seams together.
8 Turn in the waistline seam allowance and stitch it down. Leave a small opening for the elastic.
9 Thread the elastic through the casing and stitch the ends together.

Jogging suit   model 4

Pattern pieces

(top):	front panel, back panel, front neckline facing, back neckline facing, pocket.
Notions:	ruched lingerie elastic, small piece of fabric for applique (see introduction).

Sewing instructions:

1 Reproduce the pattern pieces. With right sides together, fold the fabric in half and pin the pieces to it, having the middle of the front and the middle of the front neckline against the fabric fold.
2 Cut out with an extra ⅜" (1cm) for seam allowance.
3 Zigzag around the edges of the pieces.
4 Reproduce the drawing for the applique and cut out in contrasting fabric. Apply fusible webbing to the back and zigzag stitch in place on the pocket. Turn in and stitch the edges of the pocket.
5 Stitch the pocket where indicated on the front panel.
6 Stitch the front neckline facing to the neckline. Clip the seam allowance.
7 Stitch the back neckline facings to the neckline. Clip the seam allowance.

8 Stitch the upper arm seams of the facing and the front and back panels together at the same time. Turn in the facing and top-stitch around the neckline.
9 Turn in the seam allowance at the end of the sleeves and stitch stretched ruched lingerie elastic to the inside. In this way the ends of the sleeves are finished at the same time.
10 Stitch the underarm side seams. Clip the curve in the seam allowance.
11 Turn in the seam allowance at the bottom edge of the jogging top. Stitch stretched ruched lingerie elastic to the inside of the bottom edge.
12 Turn in and stitch both edges of the back panels.
13 Stitch pieces of hook and eye fastening band to the back panel.

Pattern pieces

(pants):	pants front, pants back
Notions:	ruched lingerie elastic ⅜" (1cm) wide, elastic for the waistline

Sewing instructions:

Follow the sewing instructions for model 3. The only variation is in step 6.

6 Turn in the seam allowance at the ends of the legs and stitch stretched ruched lingerie elastic to the inside.

Jogging suit (alternative top)

Place the pattern for the front of the jogging top on a sheet of folded paper. Place the middle of the front against the paper fold. Cut out the pattern. Open it and draw a diagonal line from the bottom right-hand corner to the left shoulder. Cut across the pattern. Cut out the two sections in two different fabrics.

Use model 4 for the rest of the pattern and sewing instructions. Omit all references to the pocket.

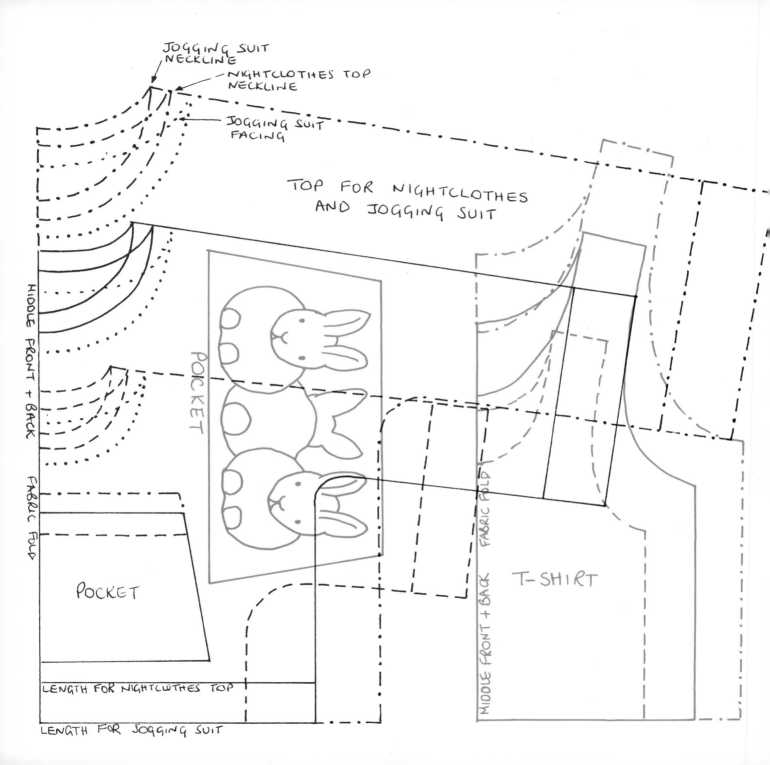

JOGGING SUIT
NECKLINE

NIGHTCLOTHES TOP
NECKLINE

JOGGING SUIT
FACING

TOP FOR NIGHTCLOTHES
AND JOGGING SUIT

MIDDLE FRONT + BACK

FABRIC FOLD

POCKET

POCKET

LENGTH FOR NIGHTCLOTHES TOP

LENGTH FOR JOGGING SUIT

T-SHIRT

MIDDLE FRONT + BACK

FABRIC FOLD

Bathrobe

model 5

Pattern pieces: front panel, back panel, front panel facing, back panel facing.

Sewing instructions:

1 Reproduce the pattern pieces on 2 x 2" (5 x 5cm) dressmaker's pattern paper. With right sides together, fold the fabric in half. Pin the pieces to it, having the middle back and back neckline facing on the fabric fold.

2 Cut out the pieces with an extra ⅜" (1cm) for seam allowance. For the tie belt cut out a strip of fabric measuring 12 x ¾" (30 x 2cm), 16 x 1" (40 x 2.5cm) or 20 x 1¼" (50 x 3cm), according to size.

3 Zigzag around the edges of the pieces.

4 Stitch the upper arm seams.

5 Stitch the shoulder seams of the back neckline facing and the front facing.

6 Stitch the facing all the way around the front and the neckline. Clip the curve in the seam allowance. Turn the robe and the facing right side out and top-stitch all the way around twice.

7 Turn in and stitch the seam allowance at the end of the sleeves.

8 Stitch the underarm side seams. Clip the curve in the seam allowance.

133

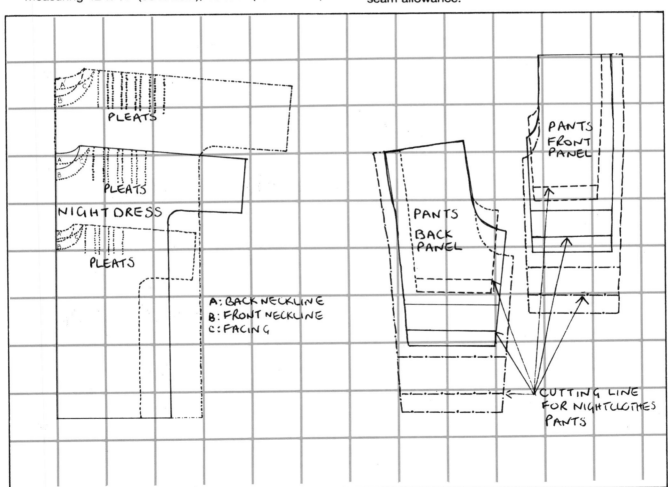

PLEATS

PLEATS

NIGHT DRESS

PLEATS

A: BACK NECKLINE
B: FRONT NECKLINE
C: FACING

PANTS BACK PANEL

PANTS FRONT PANEL

CUTTING LINE FOR NIGHTCLOTHES PANTS

9 Turn in and stitch the bottom edge of the bathrobe. Stitch it once again.
10 Press in the seam allowance all the way around the belt. Fold the belt in half lengthwise, press it flat and stitch all the way around the edge.

Short jacket

model 6

Pattern pieces: front panel, back panel, front panel facing, back neckline facing.

Sewing instructions:
1 Reproduce the pattern pieces. With right sides together, fold the fabric in half and pin the pieces to it having the middle back and the back neckline facing against the fabric fold.
2 Cut out with an extra ⅜″ (1cm) for seam allowance.

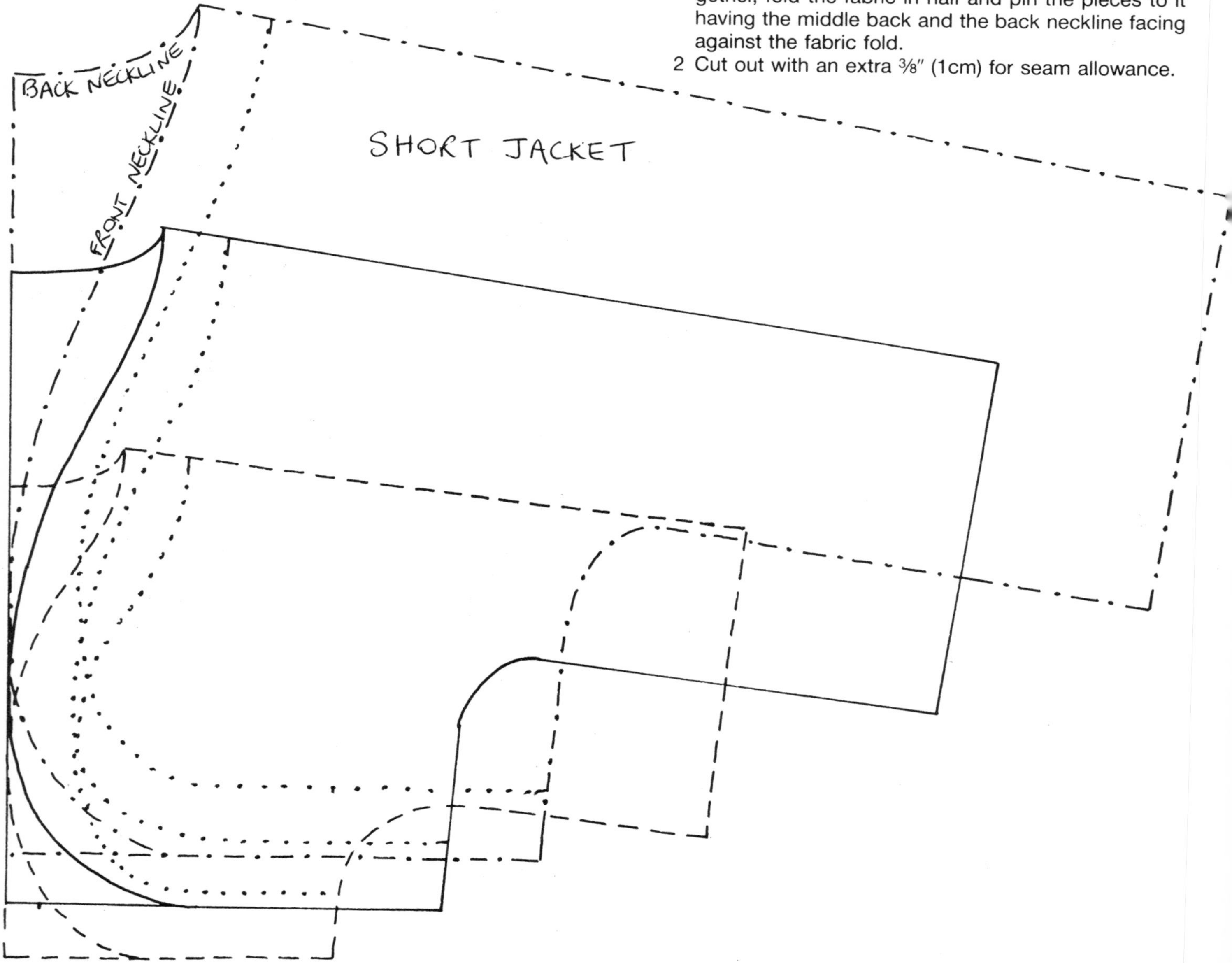

BACK NECKLINE

FRONT NECKLINE

SHORT JACKET

3 Zigzag around the edges of the pieces.
4 Stitch the upper arm seams.
5 Stitch the shoulder seams of the back neckline facing
  and the shoulder seams of the front panel facing.
6 Stitch the facing from the side seam along the front
  panel and the neckline. Clip the seam allowance and
  turn the right side out. Top-stitch all the way around.
7 Turn in and stitch the seam allowance at the bottom
  end of the sleeves.
8 Turn in the seam allowance on the bottom edge of the
  back panel.
9 Stitch the underarm side seams. In doing so, the facing
  is stitched with the side seam.

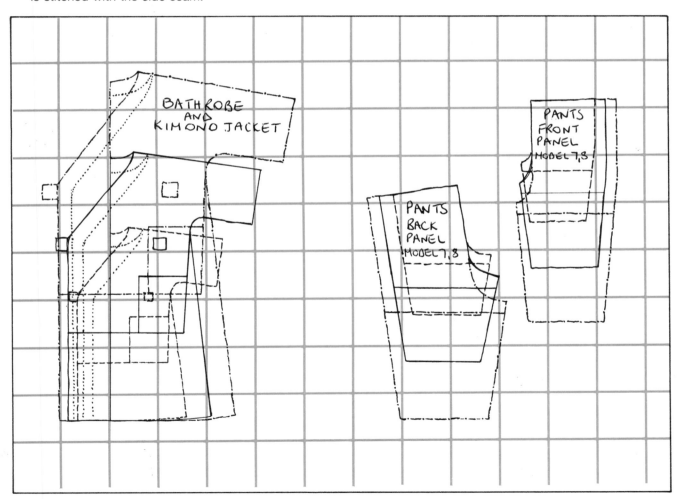

Pants
model 6

Pattern pieces: pants front, pants back
Notions: ruched lingerie elastic ⅜″ (1cm) wide

Sewing instructions:
Follow the instructions for the model 3 pants. The only variations are in steps 6 and 8. Step 9 is omitted.
6 Turn in and stitch the seam allowance at the ends of the legs.
8 Turn in and stitch the seam allowance on the waistline and stitch stretched ruched lingerie elastic to the inside. In doing so the waistline seam is finished at the same time.

Kimono jacket
model 7

Pattern pieces: front panel, back panel, front panel facing, back neckline facing, tab, pocket.
Notions: hook and eye fastening band or snap fasteners

Sewing instructions:
1 Reproduce the pattern pieces. With right sides together, fold the fabric in half and pin the pieces to it, having the middle of the back and back neckline facing against the fabric fold. Mark the positions of the pocket and the tabs.
2 Cut out the pieces with an extra ⅜″ (1cm) for seam allowance. Cut out the tab twice.
3 Zigzag around the edges of the pieces.
4 Stitch the shoulder seams of the back neckline facing and the front facing.
5 Stitch the upper arm seams.
6 Stitch the tabs together on three sides. Clip the corners and turn them right side out.
7 Stitch the facing around the front and the neckline. Stitch on both tabs where indicated. Clip the curve of the seam allowance and clip the corners diagonally. Turn the jacket and the facing right side out and top-stitch all the way around.
8 Turn in and stitch the seam allowance at the bottom edge of the sleeves.
9 Press in the seam allowance on one side edge and the top edge of the pocket. Stitch the top edge. Stitch the side edge to the jacket.
10 Stitch the underarm side seams, at the same time stitching in the other side of the pocket. Clip the curve in the seam allowance.

11 Turn in the seam allowance on the bottom edge of the jacket and pocket and stitch it down.

Pants: Follow instructions for model 6 pants.

Striped sweater
model 7

First see introduction for instructions about stitches used and size of knitting needles.

Cast on: 34, 42, 50 stitches, according to size.
Knit 4, 5, 6 rows in rib stitch.
Continue knitting in stocking stitch, 2 rows black, 2 rows white, 2 rows black etc.
Knit to a length of 1½″ (4cm), 2¼″ (5.5cm), 2¾″ (7cm).
Continue knitting in the main shade in rib stitch to a length of 2″ (5cm), 2½″ (6.5cm), 3″ (8cm).
Cast off.
Sew up the seam. This will be at the back.
Crochet or buy cords and sew these to the front and the back for shoulder straps.

Sweat-shirt for your child
model 4

Size by age: *1½ years, 3 years, 5 years*
Height of child: *34″ (86cm), 38″ (98cm), 43″ (110cm)*

Pattern pieces: front panel, back panel, front neckline facing, back neckline facing, pocket.
Fabric needed: 54″ (140cm) wide: 1⅛yd (1m)
Notions: 1⅝yd (1.50m) elastic ⅜″ (1cm) wide applique: see introduction

Sewing instructions:
1 Reproduce the pattern on 2 x 2″ (5 x 5cm) dressmaker's pattern paper.
2 With right sides together fold the fabric in half and pin the pieces to it, having both pieces against the fold.
3 Cut out the bottom edge of the sweat-shirt and the bottom edge of the sleeves with an extra 1″ (2.5cm) for seam allowance. The remaining edges with an extra ⅜-¾″ (1-2cm) for seam allowance.
4 Zigzag around the edges of the pieces.
5 Press in the seam allowance all the way around the pocket. Stitch the sides and stitch on the pocket where indicated.

6 Stitch the underarm side seams together. Clip the curve in the seam allowance and press the seams open.
7 Stitch the upper arm seams together. In both seams leave a 2¼" (6cm) opening at the neckline. Press the seams open. Stitch along the edges of the openings.
8 Stitch the front neckline facing to the front neckline and the back neckline facing to the back neckline. Clip the seam allowance. Press the seams open. Turn in the facings on the neckline and stitch around the neckline at the front and the back, stitching the openings at the same time. Stitch on a loop on one side of the openings. Sew a button on the other side.
9 Turn in 1" (2.5cm) on the bottom edge of the sleeves and stitch ⅝" (1.5cm) from the bottom edge, leaving a small opening. Thread elastic into this opening. Stitch the two ends of elastic together and stitch up the opening.
10 Turn in the bottom edge of the sweat-shirt and stitch ⅝" (1.5cm) from the bottom edge, leaving a small opening. Thread elastic into the opening. Stitch both ends of elastic together and stitch up the opening.

Pants for your child

Size by age: 1½ years, 3 years, 5 years
Height of child: 34" (86cm), 38" (98cm), 48" (110cm)

Pattern pieces: pants front, pants back
Fabric needed: 36" (90cm) wide: 2¼yd (2m)
54" (140cm) wide: 1⅛yd (1m)
Notions: 1⅜yd (1.20m) elastic ⅜" (1cm) wide.
For pants with elasticated ankles ⅝yd (0.5m) extra.

Sewing instructions:
1 Reproduce the pattern pieces on 2 x 2" (5 x 5cm) dressmaker's pattern paper.
2 Fold the fabric in half and pin the pieces to it. Cut out an extra 2" (5cm) for seam allowance along the top edge of the pants. At the end of the legs allow an extra 1" (2.5cm) for seam allowance. The remaining edges an extra ⅜-¾" (1-2cm) for seam allowance. If making pants with elasticated ankles, cut the bottom edge of the trouser legs 2¾" (7cm) longer.
3 Zigzag around the edges of the pieces.
4 Stitch the inside leg seams of the front and back panels together. Press the seams open.

5 Stitch the crotch seams together, leaving 1½" (4cm) open at the back. Clip the curve in the seam allowance. Press the seam open.
6 Stitch the side seams together and press them open.
7 Turn in 1" (2.5cm) along the bottom edge of the legs and stitch ¾" (2cm) from the bottom edge. For pants with elasticated ankles, leave a small opening and thread the elastic into this. Stitch the two ends together and stitch up the opening.
8 Turn in 2" (5cm) along the top edge of the pants. Stitch down ⅜" (1cm) from the top edge. Stitch once again 1" (2.5cm) from the top edge and again 1½" (4cm) from the top edge. Thread elastic into the two casings. Stitch the ends of the elastic together.

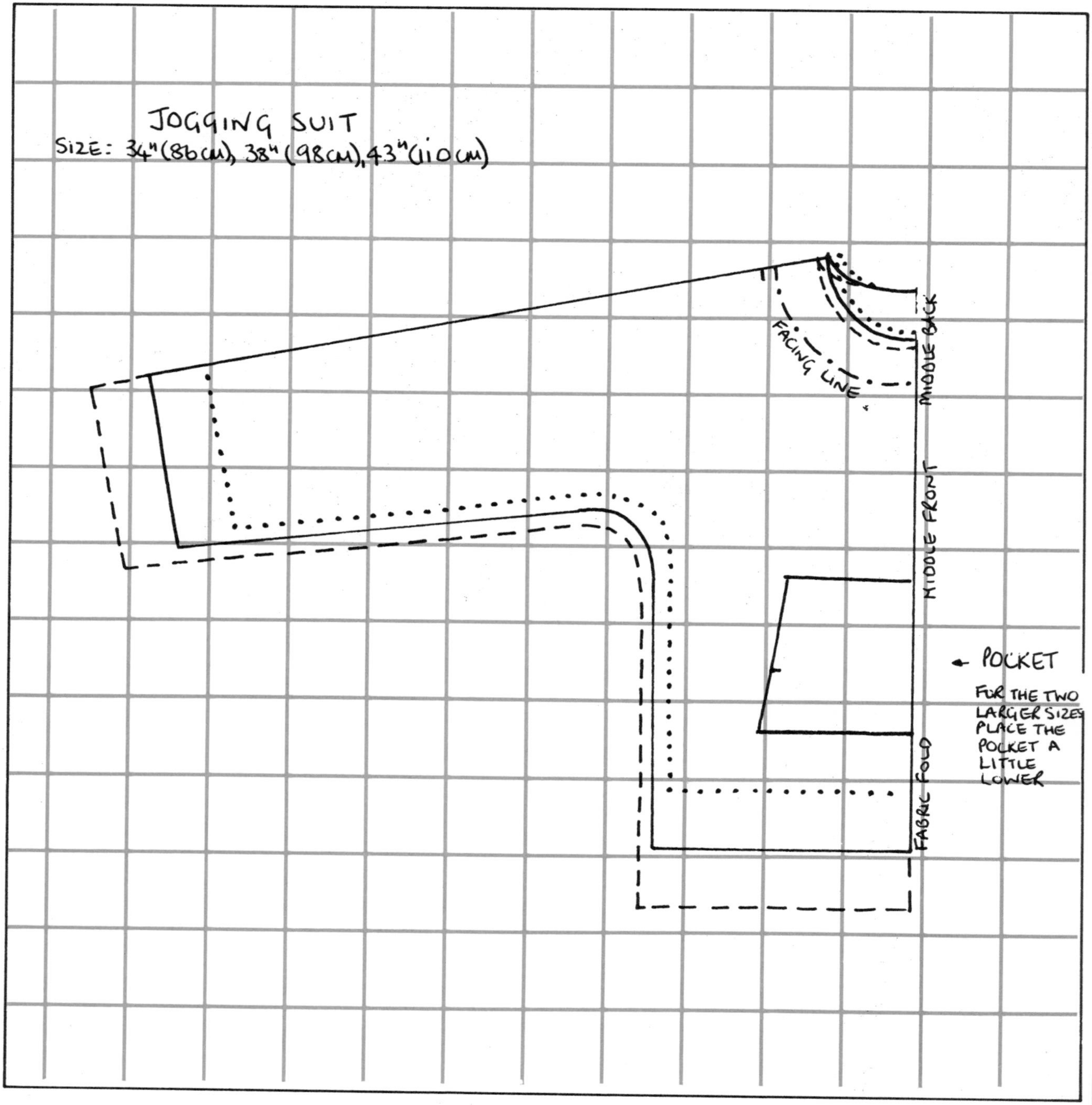

JOGGING SUIT
SIZE: 34"(86cm), 38"(98cm), 43"(110cm)

138

FACING LINE

MIDDLE BACK

MIDDLE FRONT

FABRIC FOLD

← POCKET

FOR THE TWO
LARGER SIZES
PLACE THE
POCKET A
LITTLE
LOWER

PANTS

SIZE: 34"(86cm), 38"(98cm),
43"(110cm)

FRONT
PANEL

PANTS

SIZE: 34"(86cm) 38"(98cm),
43"(110cm)

BACK
PANEL

139

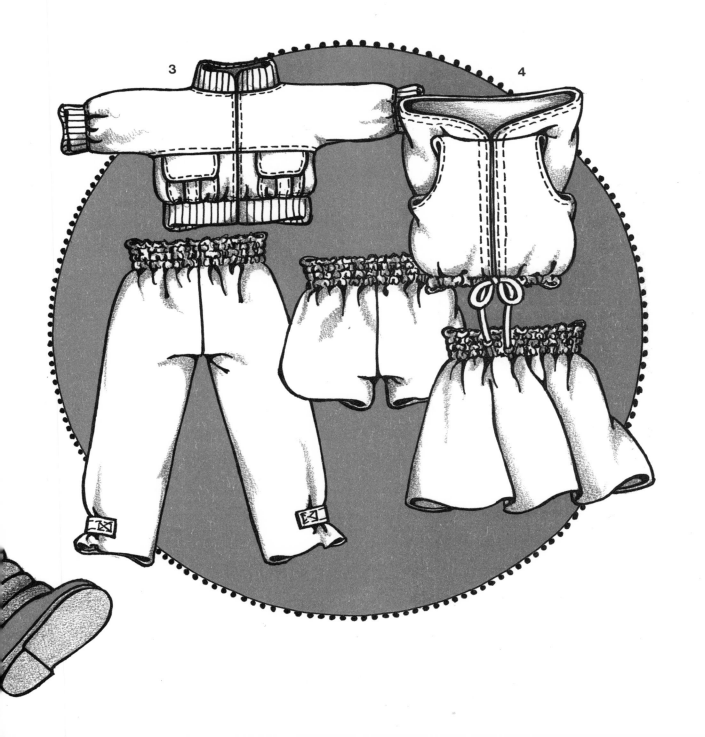

Jacket, sleeveless jacket, pants, skirt and pullover

Jacket with hood   *model 1*

Pattern pieces: front panel, back panel, hood, pocket.
Notions: hook and eye fastening band or ruched lingerie elastic ⅜″ (1cm) wide, cord.

Sewing instructions:
1 Reproduce the pattern pieces. With right sides together, fold the fabric in half and pin the pieces to it, having the middle of the back against the fabric fold.
2 Cut out an extra ¾″ (2cm) for seam allowance along the bottom edge. The remaining edges with a seam allowance of ⅜″ (1cm). Cut out the hood once again in lining fabric.
3 Zigzag around the edges of the pieces.
4 Stitch the upper arm seams.
5 Turn in the seam allowance at the bottom edge of the sleeves and stitch stretched ruched lingerie elastic to the inside.
6 Press in and stitch the seam allowance along the diagonal upper edge of the pocket. Press in the remaining seam allowances and stitch the pocket on where indicated.
7 Stitch the underarm side seams and clip the curve in the seam allowance.
8 Stitch the hood sections together. Clip the seam allowance.
9 Stitch the hood lining sections together. Clip the seam allowance.
10 Stitch the hood to the neckline. Clip the seam allowance.
11 Stitch the front edges of the hoods together. Clip the seam allowance of the neckline of the lining. Turn this in and sew the bottom edge to the neckline. Turn in

the seam allowance along the middle of the front and stitch all the way around the front of the hood. Stitch again. Turn in the seam allowance along the bottom edge and stitch ⅜″ or ⅝″ (1 or 1.5cm) from the bottom edge. Stitch pieces of hook and eye fastening band down the front opening, from the stitching for the hem to the neckline. Stitch twice, so that the stitching joins up with the stitching on the hood. Thread a cord through the casing on the bottom edge.

Sleeveless jacket   *model 2*

Pattern pieces: front panel, back panel
Notions: bias binding

Sewing instructions: Use those for baby bolero-type jacket, page 75.

Pants   *model 2*

Pattern pieces: pants front, pants back
Notions: ruched lingerie elastic ⅜″ (1cm) wide

Pattern and sewing instructions: Follow instructions for pants model 4 page 131.

Jacket with knitted cuffs   *model 3*

Pattern pieces: top section front panel, bottom section front panel, top section back panel, bottom section back panel, pocket, pocket flap, pocket tabs.
Notions: hook and eye fastening band, knitted cuffs, snap fasteners.

Sewing instructions:
1 Reproduce the pattern pieces. With right sides together fold the fabric in half and pin the pieces to it, having the top and bottom section of the back panel against the fabric fold. Cut out the pocket flaps twice.
2 Cut out the pieces with an extra ⅜″ (1cm) for seam allowance.
3 Zigzag around the edges of the pieces.
4 Stitch the upper arm seams.
5 Stitch the bottom section of the back panel to the top section of the back panel.
6 Stitch the pockets on the bottom section of the front panel.

7 With right sides together stitch two pocket flaps together. Clip the seam allowance and turn the right side out. Repeat with the other two flaps.
8 Stitch the bottom section of the front panel to the top section of the front panel. Stitch on the pocket flaps at the same time.
9 Stitch knitted cuffs to the ends of the sleeves.
10 Stitch the underarm side seams and clip the curve in the seam allowance.
11 Turn in and stitch the middle front edges.
12 Stitch the knitted cuff to the neckline.
13 Turn in and stitch the seam allowance on the pocket tabs.
14 Stitch the knitted cuff to the bottom edge of the jacket. Stitch the pocket tabs on at the same time.
15 Stitch pieces of hook and eye fastening band to the front.
16 Sew snap fasteners to the underside of the pocket flaps and the upper side of the tabs.

Sleeveless jacket model 4

Pattern pieces: front panel, back panel, hood.
Notions: hook and eye fastening band, cord.

Sewing instructions:
Follow the sewing instructions for model 1. There is a variation to step 5. Step 6 is omitted.
  5 Stitch bias binding or a facing around the armholes.

Pants model 5

Pattern pieces: pants front, pants back, see model 2.
Notions: ruched lingerie elastic ⅜″ (1cm) wide.

Pattern and sewing instructions: Use those for pants model 7 page 135/136. The tabs at the ends of the legs are stitched on at the same time as the side seam is stitched.

Shorts model 6

Pattern pieces: front panel, back panel.
Notions: ruched lingerie elastic ⅜″ (1cm) wide.

Pattern and sewing instructions: Use those for pants model 7 page 135/136.

Skirt model 7

Pattern pieces: skirt front, skirt back.
Notions: ruched lingerie elastic ⅜″ (1cm) wide.

Sewing instructions:
1 Reproduce the pattern pieces. Wtih right sides together, fold the fabric in half and pin the pieces to it, having both pieces against the fabric fold.
2 Cut out with an extra ⅜″ (1cm) for seam allowance.
3 Zigzag around the edges of the pieces.
4 Stitch one side seam and press open.
5 Turn in and stitch the bottom edge.
6 Turn in the top edge and stitch stretched ruched lingerie elastic to the inside.
7 Stitch the other side seam.

Turtle-neck pullover

First see introduction for instructions about stitches used and size of knitting needles.

Front panel
Cast on: 28, 34, 40 stitches, according to size.
Knit 4, 5, 6 rows in rib stitch.
Continue in stocking stitch, and increase 4, 4, 6 stitches on the first row.
Knit to a length of 4″ (10cm), 5″ (13cm), 6¼″ (16cm).
Put the middle 8, 12, 14 stitches on a reserve strand.
Continue knitting on both sides and every other row pick up 1 stitch on the reserve strand. 1, 2, 2 stitches respectively.
Knit to a length of 4½″ (11.5cm), 6″ (15cm), 7½″ (19cm).
Cast off the shoulder stitches or put them on a reserve strand.

Left back panel
Cast on: 16, 20, 22 stitches, according to size.
Knit 4, 5, 6 rows in rib stitch.
Continue in stocking stitch, but knit the first 4 stitches on the right-hand side in rib stitch. Increase 1, 2, 3 stitches on the first row.
Knit to 4¼″ (10.5cm), 6¼″ (15.5cm), 6½″ (16.5cm).
Pick up 7, 8, 9 stitches from the right-hand side on a reserve strand.
Every other row pick up 1 stitch on a reserve strand. 1, 2, 2 stitches respectively.
When you have knitted to a length of 4½″ (11.5cm), 6″

(15cm), 7½" (19cm), pick up the shoulder stitches on a reserve strand or cast them off.

Right back panel
As for the left but in reverse.

Sleeve
Cast on: 20, 22, 24 stitches.
Knit 3, 4, 5 rows in rib stitch.
Continue in stocking stitch.
Increase 2, 4, 4 stitches on the first row.
Knit to 2¼" (6cm), 2¾" (7cm), 3¼" (8cm). Cast off.

Construction
Baste or sew the shoulder seams together.
Pick up 36, 45 or 54 stitches at the neckline, including the stitches from the reserve strand of wool.
Continue to knit in rib stitch to 1¼" (3cm), 1¾" (4.5cm), 2¼" (6cm). Cast off.
Sew on the sleeves, having the middle of the top against the shoulder seam.
Sew the underarm side seams together.
Sew snap fasteners or hook and eye fastening band to the back opening.

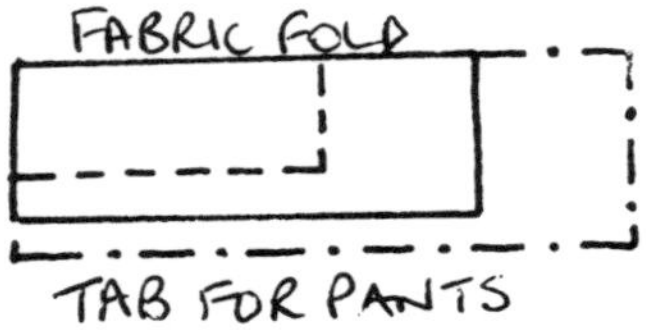

FABRIC FOLD

TAB FOR PANTS

WHEN TRACING JOIN THE TWO SECTIONS

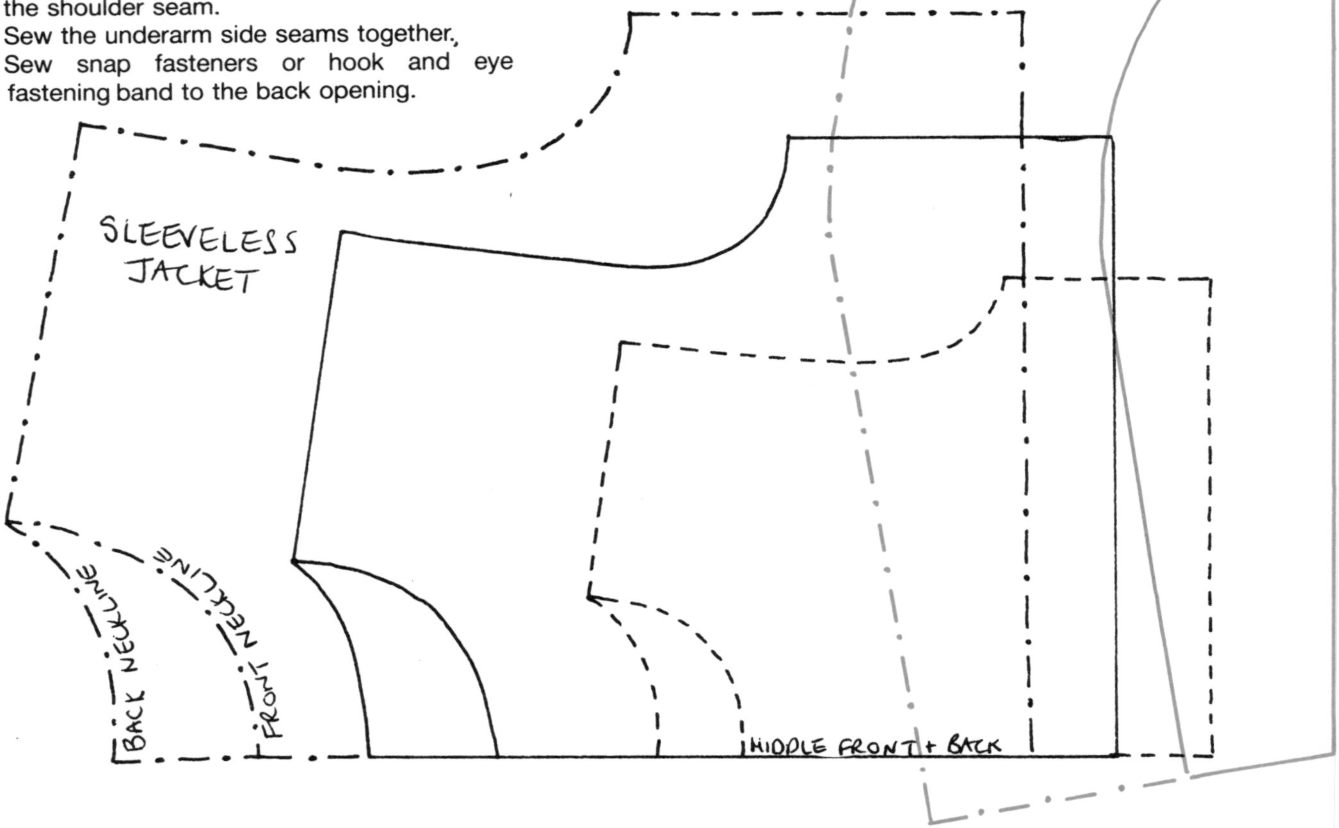

SLEEVELESS JACKET

BACK NECKLINE

FRONT NECKLINE

MIDDLE FRONT + BACK

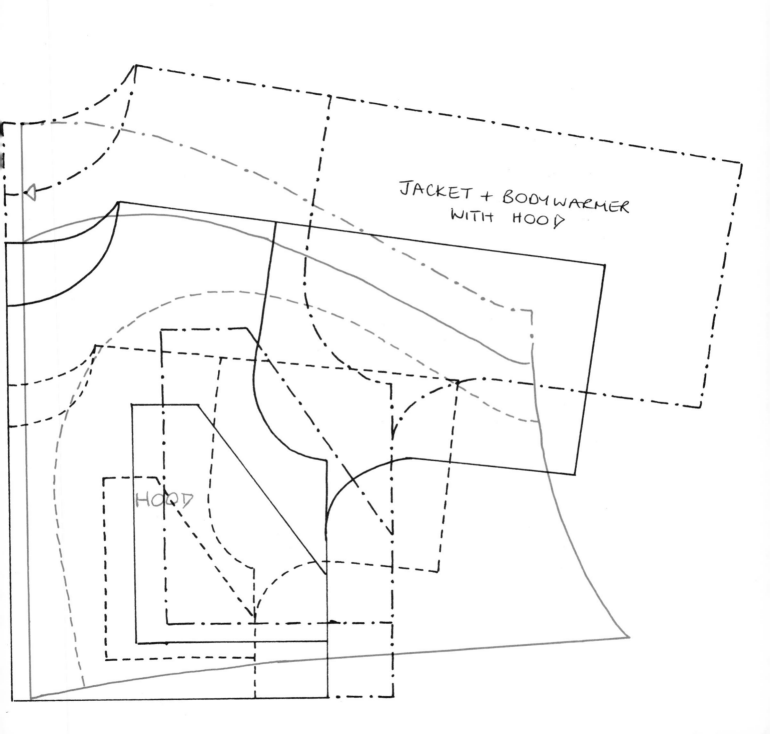

JACKET + BODYWARMER
WITH HOOD

HOOD

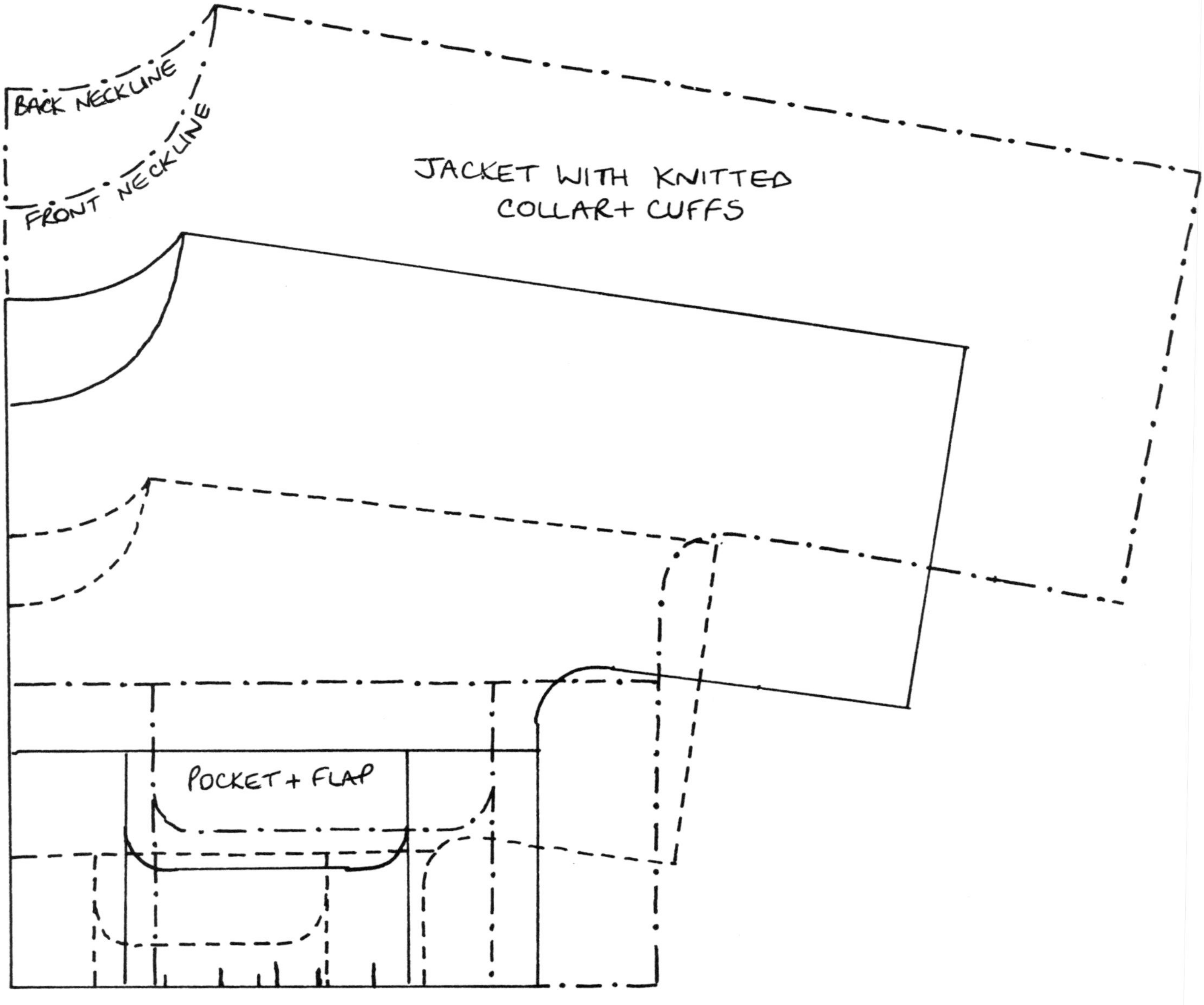

BACK NECKLINE

FRONT NECKLINE

JACKET WITH KNITTED
COLLAR + CUFFS

POCKET + FLAP

UPPER SIDE, POCKET TABS

147

TOP EDGE

FABRIC FOLD

¼ SKIRT

Bodywarmer for your child

Size by age: 3 years,   5 years,   7 years
Height of child: 38" (98cm), 43" (110cm), 47" (122cm)

Pattern pieces: front panel, back panel, hood.
Fabric needed: 36" (90cm) wide: 1¼yd (1.10m)
               54" (140cm) wide: ¾yd (0.7m)
Lining: 36" (90cm) wide: 1¼yd (1.10m)
               54" (140cm) wide: ¾yd (0.7m)
Notions: 18" (46cm) zipper, 1¾yds (1.5m) cord

148

Sewing instructions:

1 Reproduce the pattern pieces on 2 x 2" (5 x 5cm) dressmaker's pattern paper. Mark the position of the pockets and the casing.
2 With right sides together fold the fabric in half and pin the pieces to it, having the middle of the back and the casing against the fabric fold.
3 Cut out the middle of the front with an extra ¾" (2cm) for seam allowance. Cut out the remaining edges with an extra ⅜-¾" (1-2cm) for seam allowance.
4 Cut out the front panel, back panel and hood in lining fabric. Do this in the same way.
5 Zigzag around the edges of the pieces.
6 Stitch the side seams together. Press them open.
7 Stitch the shoulder seams together.
8 Stitch the hood sections together. Clip the seam allowance and press the seam open.
9 Stitch the hood to the neckline. Clip the seam allowance and press the seam open.
10 Repeat steps 6, 7, 8 with the lining sections.
11 With right sides together, fit the jackets into each other. Stitch the armholes and the front of the hood together. Turn the jacket right side out.
12 Press in the seam allowance along the middle front of the jacket. Do the same with the lining fabric. Baste the zipper between the two fabrics and stitch in place. (See introduction for how to insert zipper.) Carry on stitching around the front edge of the hood. Leave an opening at the bottom and thread cord through.
13 Top-stitch around the armholes ⅜" (1cm) from the edge.
14 Turn in the bottom edge of both fabrics and stitch both layers together ¼" (0.5cm) from the bottom edge. Stitch again ¾" (2cm) from the bottom edge.
15 Thread cord through the casing.

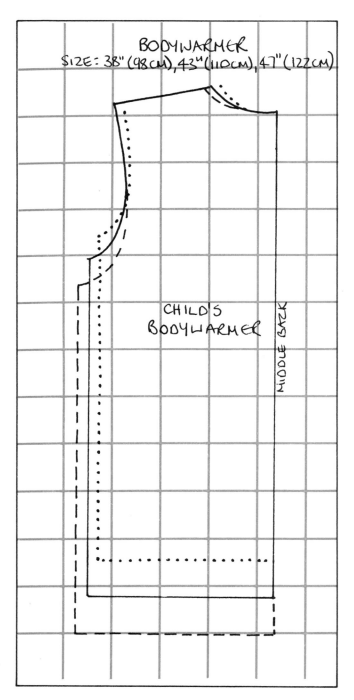

BODYWARMER
SIZE: 38" (98cm), 43" (110cm), 47" (122cm)

CHILD'S BODYWARMER

MIDDLE BACK

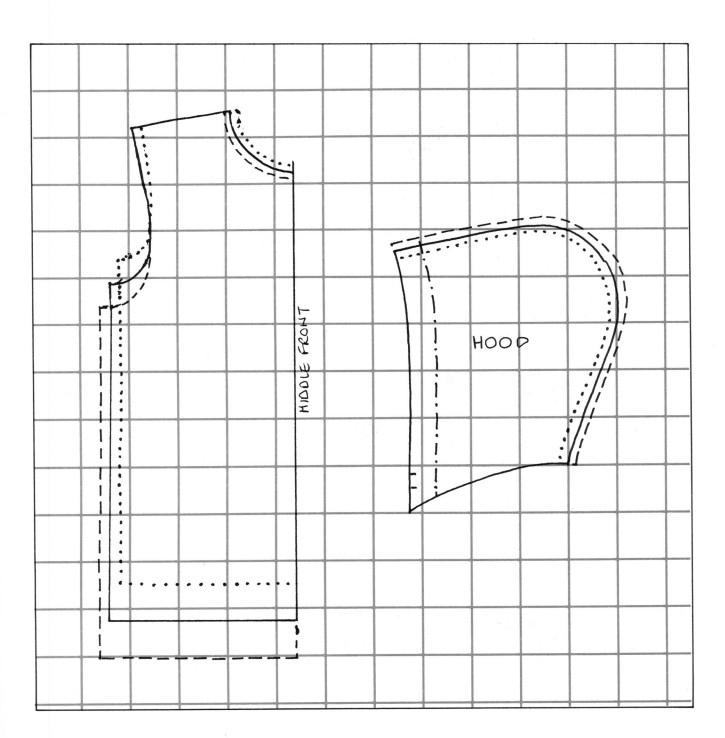

MIDDLE FRONT

HOOD

Overalls, skirt with bib top, all-in-one suit, skirt, bolero-type jacket

Overalls *model 1*

Pattern pieces: front panel, back panel, shoulder strap, front pocket, side pocket.
Notions: ruched lingerie elastic ⅜″ (1cm) wide, buttons.

Sewing instructions:
1 Reproduce the pattern pieces on 2 x 2″ (5 x 5cm) dressmaker's pattern paper. With right sides together fold the fabric in half and pin the pieces to it, having the top pocket and the shoulder strap against the fabric fold. Mark the positions of the pockets, the loop and the ruched lingerie elastic.
2 Cut out the pieces with an extra ⅜″ (1cm) for seam allowance.
3 Zigzag around the edges of the pieces.
4 Stitch the inside leg seams of the pants front and the pants back together.
5 Stitch the middle front and the middle back together all the way around. Clip the curve in the seam allowance and press the seam to one side. Stitch the seam down.
6 Fold the shoulder straps in half lengthwise and stitch them. Turn them right side out. Leave the diagonal side open. Top-stitch around the edges.
7 Turn in the seam allowance along the top edge of the back panel and stitch the top edge at ¼″ (0.5cm) from the edge. Stitch on the shoulder straps at the same time – the diagonal side is stitched to the back panel.
8 Turn in the seam allowance on the top edge of the front panel and stitch ¼″ (0.5cm) from the edge.
9 Turn in and stitch the seam allowance on the side of the top pocket.

10 Turn in and stitch the seam allowance on the edge of the side pocket which is to be the opening.
11 Turn in and pin the seam allowances on the sides of the pockets. The seam allowance on the top edge of the side pocket is placed under the bottom edge of the top pocket. The seam allowance on the side edge of the side pocket will be stitched with the side seam.
12 Stitch both pockets to the front panel.
13 Stitch stretched ruched lingerie elastic to the waistline of the back panel.
14 Stitch stretched ruched lingerie elastic to the waistline of the front panel from the pocket to the side seam.
15 Turn in and stitch the seam allowance at the ends of the legs.
16 Stitch the side seams. Stitch the edge of the side pocket at the same time.
17 Make buttonholes and sew the buttons to the shoulder straps.

Skirt with bib top *model 2*

Pattern pieces: bib front panel, bib back panel, skirt front, skirt back.
Notions: bias binding

Sewing instructions:
1 Reproduce the pattern pieces. With right sides together, fold the fabric in half and pin the pieces to it, having all the pieces against the fabric fold. Mark the position of the shoulder ties, side ties and the openings.
2 Cut out the pieces with an extra ⅜″ (1cm) for seam allowance.
3 Zigzag around the edges of the pieces.
4 Turn in and stitch the seam allowance along the top edge of the bib front. Stitch on pieces of bias binding at the same time.
5 Repeat step 4 with the back bib.
6 Gather the front and the back skirt.
7 Stitch the front skirt to the front bib.
8 Stitch the back skirt to the back bib.
9 Stitch the side seams as far as the opening. Press the seams open.
10 Stitch all the way along the edges of the openings and the sides of the bibs. At the same time stitch bias binding ties on to the waistline.
11 Turn in and stitch the hemline seam allowance.

Petticoat
model 2

Pattern pieces: skirt front, skirt back.
Notions: ruched lingerie elastic ⅜″ (1cm) wide.

Sewing instructions: Use those for skirt, model 7, p143.

All-in-one suit
model 3

Pattern pieces: front panel, back panel, pocket, collar.
Notions: zipper, ruched lingerie elastic ⅜″ (1cm) wide.

Sewing instructions:
1 Reproduce the pattern pieces on 2 x 2″ (5 x 5cm) dressmaker's pattern paper. With right sides together, fold the fabric in half and pin the pieces to it, having the collar against the fabric fold. Mark the positions of the pockets.
2 Cut out the middle front with an extra ⅝″ (1.5cm) for seam allowance. The remaining edges with an extra ⅜″ (1cm) for seam allowance.
3 Zigzag around the edges of the pieces.
4 Stitch the inside leg seams of the pants front and the pants back together.
5 Stitch together the middle back seam and the lowest section of the middle front seam. Clip the curve in the seam allowance.
6 Stitch the zipper into the middle front seam. (See introduction for how to insert zipper.)
7 Turn in and stitch the seam allowance on the opening side of the pockets. Press in the seam allowances around the edges of the pockets. Place the pockets where indicated and stitch along the top, inside and bottom edges. The outer edge will be stitched in with the side seam later.
8 Stitch stretched ruched lingerie elastic where indicated on the waistline of the back panel.
9 Stitch stretched ruched lingerie elastic in the front panels stopping ⅜″ (1cm) from the zipper.
10 Stitch the upper arm seams.
11 Turn in the seam allowance at the bottom ends of the sleeves and stitch stretched ruched lingerie elastic to the insides.
12 Turn in the bottom ends of the legs and stitch stretched ruched lingerie elastic to the insides.

13 With right sides together place the collar pieces against the neckline and stitch.
14 With right sides together, place the collar facing against the collar and stitch together along the top edge. Clip the curve in the seam allowance. Turn the right sides out.
15 Clip the seam allowance of the neckline. Turn the seam allowance of the neckline and that of the collar facing into the collar and sew the facing to the neckline.
16 Top-stitch the edge of the collar.
17 Stitch the underarm side seams. Clip the curve in the seam allowance.

Gathered overalls
model 4

Pattern pieces: pants front, pants back, bib front panel, bib back panel.
Notions: bias binding.

Sewing instructions:
1 Reproduce the pattern pieces on 2 x 2″ (5 x 5cm) dressmaker's pattern paper. With right sides together, fold the fabric in half and pin the pieces to it, having the bibs against the fabric fold. Mark the position of the ties.
2 Cut out the pieces with an extra ⅜″ (1cm) for seam allowance.
3 Zigzag around the edges of the pieces.
4 Turn in and stitch the seam allowance along the top edge of the bibs. At the same time stitch on pieces of bias binding to the top edge.
5 Stitch together the inside leg seams of the pants front and the pants back.
6 Stitch the crotch seams together. Clip the seam allowance.
7 Gather the pants front and the pants back.
8 Stitch the pants front to the front bib.
9 Stitch the pants back to the back bib.
10 Gather the bottom edges of the legs and stitch bias binding around the ends. Leave a length of binding loose on each side to make a tie fastening.
11 Stitch the side seams, leaving an opening at the top and the bottom.
12 Stitch along the edges of the openings and the side edges of the bibs. At the same time, stitch pieces of bias binding on at the waistline.

Square-necked pullover

First see introduction for instructions about stitches used and size of knitting needles.

Front panel
Cast on: 28, 34, 40 stitches, according to size.
Knit 4, 5, 6 rows in rib stitch.
Continue in stocking stitch. Increase 4, 4, 5 stitches in the first row.
Knit to a length of 3" (8cm), 4¼" (11cm), 5½" (14cm). Continue in rib stitch to a length of 4" (10cm), 5" (13cm), 6¼" (16cm).
Cast off the middle 8, 12, 14 stitches.
Continue knitting on both sides to a length of 4½" (11.5cm), 6" (15cm), 7¼" (18.5cm).
Cast off the shoulder stitches or pick them up on a reserve strand.

Left back panel
Cast on: 16, 20, 22 stitches.
Knit 4, 5, 6 rows in rib stitch.
Continue in stocking stitch but knit the first 4 stitches on the right-hand side in rib stitch. Increase 1, 2, 3 stitches in the first row.
Knit to a length of 3½" (9cm), 4¾" (12cm), 6⅛" (15.5cm). Continue in rib stitch to 4¼" (11cm), 5½" (14cm), 7" (17.5cm).
Cast off 7, 8, 9 stitches from the right-hand side.
Knit with the remaining stitches to a length of 4½" (11.5cm), 6" (15cm), 7¼" (18.5cm).
Put the shoulder stitches on a reserve strand or cast them off.

Right back panel
As for the left but in reverse.

154

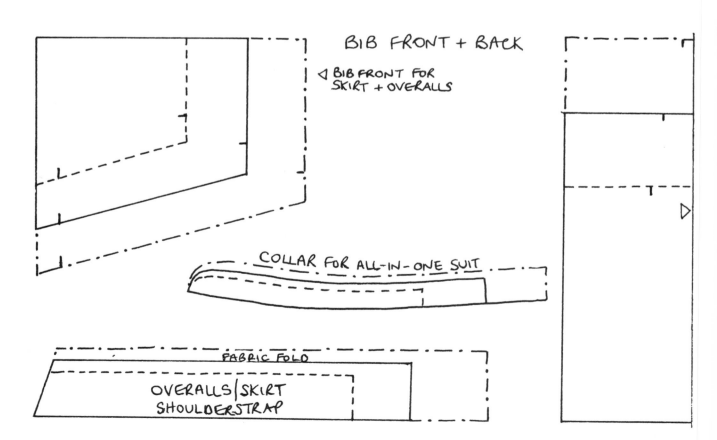

BIB FRONT + BACK

◁ BIB FRONT FOR SKIRT + OVERALLS

COLLAR FOR ALL-IN-ONE SUIT

FABRIC FOLD

OVERALLS/SKIRT SHOULDERSTRAP

Sleeve
Cast on 20, 22, 24 stitches.
Knit 3, 4, 5 rows in rib stitch.
Continue in stocking stitch. Increase 2, 4, 4 stitches in the first row.
Continue knitting to a length of 2¼" (6cm), 2¾" (7cm), 3" (8cm).
Cast off.

Construction
Sew or back-stitch the shoulder seams together. Optional: crochet a decorative border around the neckline.
Sew on the sleeves, having the middle of the upper edge against the shoulder seam.
Sew the underarm side seams together.
Sew snap fasteners or hook and eye fastening band to the back.

Knitted bolero-type jacket

First see introduction for instructions about stitches used and size of knitting needles.

Cast on 24, 32, 38 stitches, according to size.
Knit in plain stitch to a length of 2¾" (7cm), 3¼" (8.5cm), 4" (10cm). Cast off the middle 8, 10, 12 stitches.
Pick up the shoulder stitches on one side on a reserve strand.
* Continue knitting on one side to a length of 3½" (9cm), 4⅛" (10.5cm), 5" (12.5cm).
Increase 4, 5, 6 stitches on the neckline side.
Continue knitting to a total length of 6" (15cm), 7" (18cm), 8¼" (21cm). Cast off.
Using the stitches from the reserve strand repeat from * in reverse.

Construction
Sew up the lower section of the side seams.

155

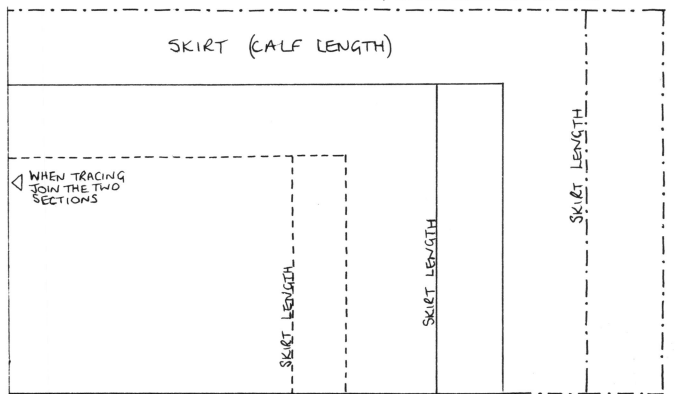

SKIRT (CALF LENGTH)

WHEN TRACING JOIN THE TWO SECTIONS

SKIRT LENGTH

SKIRT LENGTH

SKIRT LENGTH

All-in-one suit for your child

model 3

Size by age: *2 years,   4 years,   6 years*
Height of child: *36" (90cm), 40" (104cm), 45" (116cm)*

Pattern pieces: front panel, back panel, collar.
Fabric needed: 36" (90cm) wide: 5⅛yd (4.7m)
                    54" (140cm) wide: 2⅝yd (2.4m)
Notions: 16" (40cm) zipper, 20" (50cm) elastic ⅜"
                    (1cm) wide, 24" (60cm) ruched lingerie
                    elastic ¾" (2cm) wide

Sewing instructions:

1 Reproduce the pattern pieces on 2 x 2" (5 x 5cm) dressmaker's pattern paper. Mark the position of the ruched lingerie elastic on the front and the back panel.

2 With right sides together fold the fabric in half and pin the pieces to it, having the collar against the fabric fold. Cut out the collar twice, the second piece will be the collar facing.

3 Cut out the middle front with an extra ¾" (2cm) for seam allowance, the bottom edge of the sleeves with an extra 1" (2.5cm) and the bottom edge of the legs with an extra 1¼" (3cm). If you wish to make pants with elasticated ankles you will need to cut the legs 2¾" (7cm) longer.

4 Zigzag around the edges of the pieces.

5 Stitch the inside leg seams of the pants front and the pants back together. Press the seams open.

6 Stitch the middle back seam and a small section of the bottom of the middle front seam. Clip the curve in the seam allowance and press the seam open.

7 Stitch the zipper into the middle front seam (see introduction).

8 Stitch the upper arm seams. Press them open.

9 Stitch the underarm side seams. Clip the curve in the seam allowance and press them open.

10 Stitch stretched ruched lingerie elastic where indicated on the waistline. Begin ¾" (2cm) from the zipper. First measure the child's waist.

11 Stitch the collar to the neckline. Clip the seam allowance and iron the seam up.

12 With the right sides together, stitch the upper edge of the collar facing to the upper edge of the collar. Clip the curve in the seam allowance. Turn the right side out and press the seam flat. Turn in the bottom edge of the collar facing and stitch to the collar, keeping close to the neckline.

156

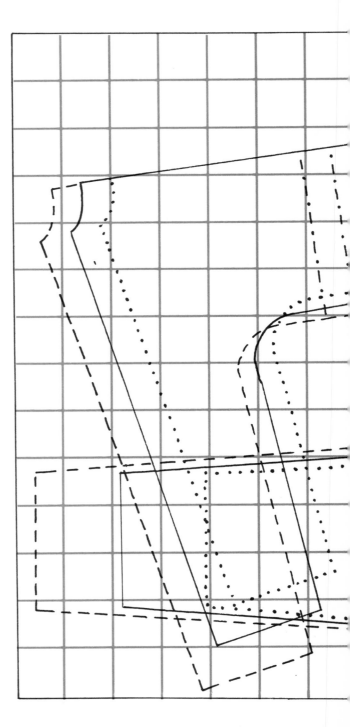

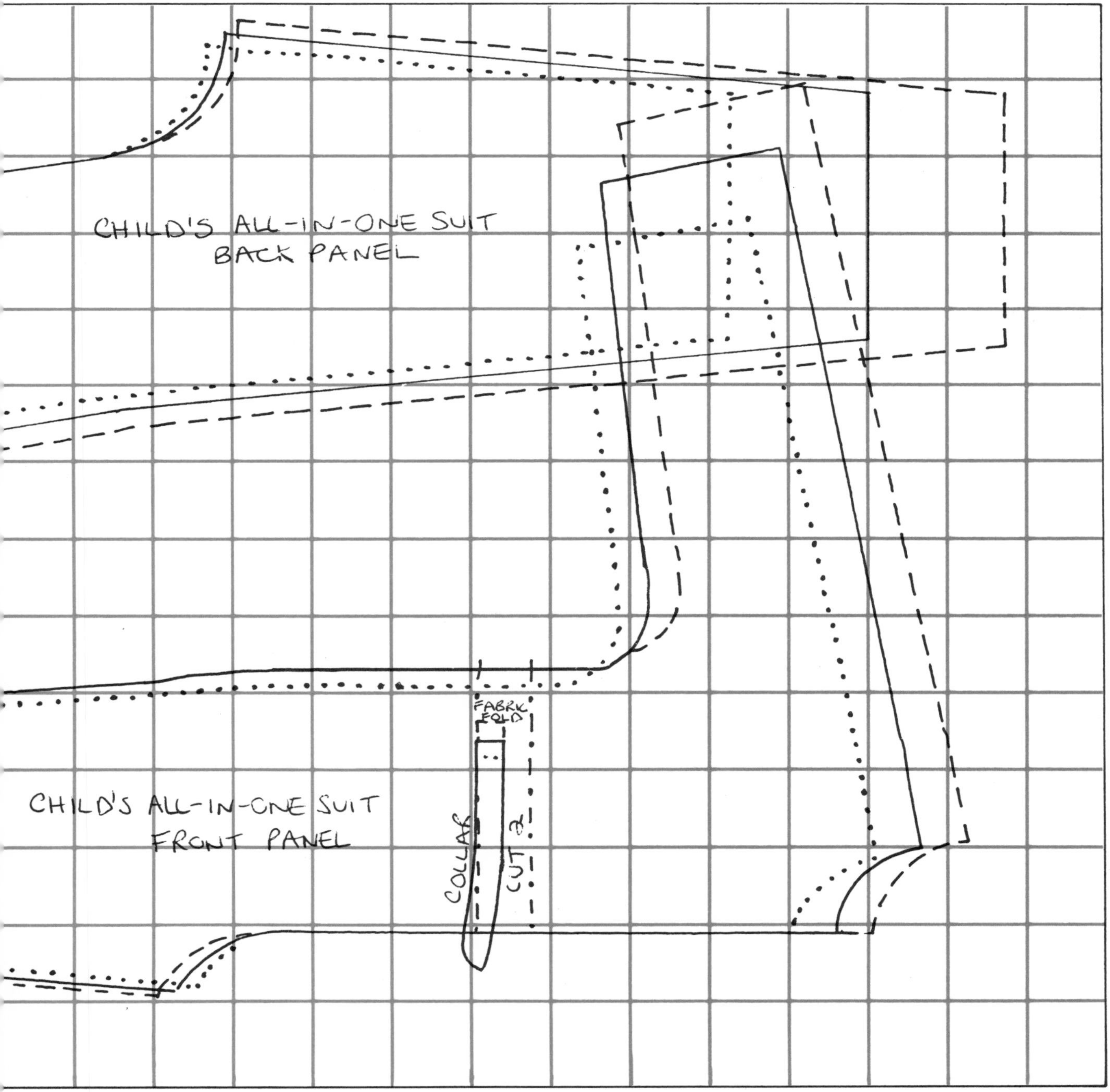

CHILD'S ALL-IN-ONE SUIT
BACK PANEL

157

CHILD'S ALL-IN-ONE SUIT
FRONT PANEL

FABRIC
FOLD

COLLAR

CUT 2

13 Starting at the stitching for the zipper, top-stitch all the way around the collar.

14 Turn in 1″ (2.5cm) along the bottom edge of the sleeves and stitch down ⅝″ (1.5cm) from the edge. Leave a small opening. Thread the elastic through the casing. Stitch the two ends of the elastic together.

15 Turn in 1¼″ (3cm) along the bottom edge of the legs. Stitch ¾″ (2cm) from the bottom edge. If the ends of the legs are to be elasticated, leave a small opening in the seam. Thread the elastic through this and stitch the ends together.

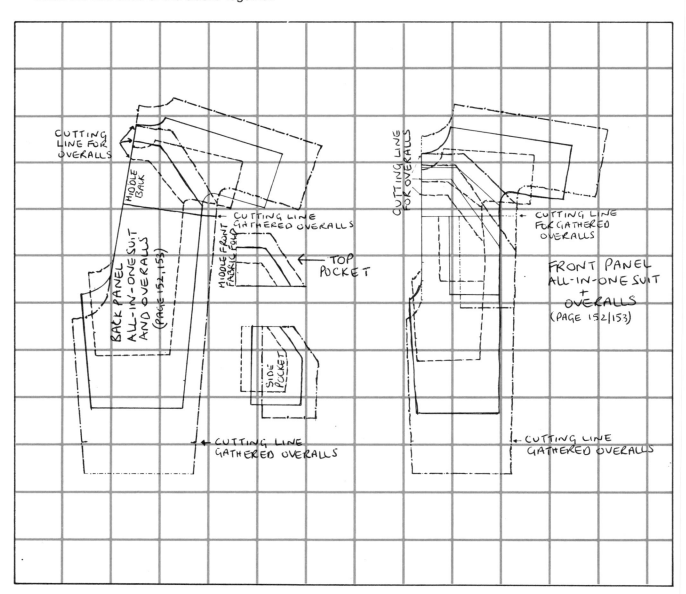

Blouse, skirt, pants and pullover

Blouse *model 1*

Pattern pieces: front panel, back panel, front neckline facing, back neckline facing. See page 131: jogging suit.

Notions: hook and eye fastening band, ruched lingerie elastic ⅜″ (1cm) wide.

Sewing instructions:
1 Reproduce the pattern pieces. With right sides together, fold the fabric in half and pin the pieces to it, having the middle of the front and the middle front facing against the fabric fold.
2 Cut out with an extra ⅜″ (1cm) for seam allowance.
3 Zigzag around the edges of the pieces.
4 Stitch the front neckline facing to the neckline. Clip the seam allowance.
5 Stitch the back neckline facings to the back neckline. Clip the seam allowance.
6 Stitch the upper arm seams. Stitch the sides of the facings at the same time. Turn in the facing and top-stitch around the neckline.
7 Turn in and stitch the bottom edge of the sleeves or turn in the seam allowance at the bottom of the sleeves and stitch stretched ruched lingerie elastic to the insides.
8 Stitch the underarm side seams. Clip the curve in the seam allowance.
9 Turn in and stitch the seam allowance on the bottom edge.
10 Turn in the seam allowance down the middle of the back and stitch pieces of hook and eye fastening band to the back opening (see introduction).

Skirt *model 2*

Pattern pieces: top section skirt front, top section skirt back, bottom section skirt front, bottom section skirt back.

Notions: ruched lingerie elastic ⅜″ (1cm) wide.

Sewing instructions:
1 Reproduce the pattern pieces. With right sides together fold the fabric in half and pin the pieces to it, having all the pieces against the fabric fold.
2 Cut out the pieces with an extra ⅜″ (1cm) for seam allowance.
3 Zigzag around the edges of the pieces.
4 Gather the bottom section of the skirt front and the bottom section of the skirt back.
5 Stitch these to the top sections.
6 Stitch one side seam and press this open.
7 Turn in the waistline edge and stitch stretched ruched lingerie elastic to the inside.
8 Stitch the remaining side seam together.
9 Turn in and stitch the hemline.

Pants *model 3*

Pattern pieces: pants front, pants back, pockets.

Notions: ruched lingerie elastic ⅜″ (1cm) wide.

Pattern and sewing instructions: Use nightclothes pants model 3, pages 130 and 133.

Pattern and sewing instructions for pockets: Use all-in-one suit, pages 153 and 158.

Pullover

First see introduction for instructions about stitches used and size of knitting needles.

Front panel
Cast on: 26, 30, 34 stitches, according to size.
Knit 4, 5, 6 rows in rib stitch.
Continue in stocking stitch. Increase 4, 4, 5 stitches in the first row.
Optional: knit the following rows in jacquard pattern.
When you have knitted to a length of 2″ (5cm), 2¼″ (6cm), 2¾″ (7cm), knit 4, 4, 4 stitches on both sides in rib stitch in the main shade.

FABRIC FOLD

¼ TOP SECTION SKIRT

FABRIC FOLD

¼ BOTTOM SECTION
SKIRT FRONT + BACK

Continue knitting the stitches in between in stocking stitch (or jacquard pattern) to 3¼″ (8cm), 4″ (10cm), 4¼″ (11cm).
Now continue knitting all stitches in rib stitch in the main shade to a length of 4″ (10cm), 4¾″ (12cm), 5″ (13cm). Cast off the middle 8, 12, 14 stitches.
Continue knitting on both sides to a length of 4¾″ (12cm), 5¾″ (14.5cm), 6¼″ (16cm).
Cast off the shoulder stitches or put them on a reserve strand.

Left back panel
Cast on: 14, 16, 18 stitches.
Knit 4, 5, 6 rows in rib stitch.
Continue in stocking stitch, but knit the first 4 stitches on the right-hand side in rib stitch. Increase 1, 2, 3 stitches in the first row.
Optional: knit the following rows in jacquard pattern. In that case continue to knit the first 4 stitches on the right-hand side in the main shade.
When your knitting measures 2″ (5cm), 2¼″ (6cm), 2¾″ (7cm), knit 4, 4, 4 stitches in rib stitch on the left-hand side in the main shade. Knit the stitches in between in stocking stitch (or in jacquard pattern) to a length of 3½″ (9cm), 4¼″ (11cm), 5″ (12.5cm).
Continue to knit all the stitches in rib stitch in the main shade to a length of 4¼″ (11cm), 5⅛″ (13cm), 5¾″ (14.5cm). Cast off 7, 8, 9 stitches on the right-hand side.
Continue knitting the remaining stitches to a length of 4¾″ (12cm), 5¾″ (14.5cm), 6¼″ (16cm).
Put the shoulder stitches on a reserve strand or cast them off.
Make the right-hand back panel the same as the left but in reverse.

Construction
Sew or back-stitch the shoulder seams together. Optional: crochet a border around the neckline.
Sew the side seams together as far as the cuff for the armhole.
Sew snap fasteners or hook and eye fastening band to the back.

Skirt for your child

Size by age:	3 years,	5 years,	7 years
Height of child:	38″ (98cm),	43″ (110cm),	47″ (122cm)

Pattern pieces: skirt front, skirt back, top section skirt front, top section skirt back.
Fabric needed: 36″ (90cm) wide: 1⅝yd (1.5m)
54″ (140cm) wide: ¾yd (0.7m)
Notions: 25½″ (65cm) elastic for each casing.

Sewing instructions:
1 Reproduce the pattern pieces on 2 x 2″ (5 x 5cm) dressmaker's pattern paper.
2 With right sides together, fold the fabric in half and pin the pieces to it. Depending on the width of the fabric, pin either the middle back or middle front against the fabric fold, or pin both the middle back and the middle front against the fold. Pin both top sections against the fabric fold.
3 Cut out with an extra ⅜″ (1cm) for seam allowance. Cut out an additional 2″ (5cm) seam allowance along the top edge of the top sections.
4 Zigzag around the edges of the pieces.
5 Stitch all side seams. On one side leave the extra seam allowance on the top section open.
6 Fold in the extra seam allowance along the top section and stitch around it to form casings.
7 Gather the bottom section of the skirt until it is the same width as the top section.
8 Stitch the bottom section to the top section.
9 Turn in and stitch the hemline.
10 Thread elastic through the casings.

STITCHING LINES
FOR CASINGS

FABRIC FOLD

TOP SECTION
CUT 2

GATHER

BOTTOM SECTION
SKIRT FRONT + BACK

FABRIC FOLD

CUT 2

SKIRT
SIZE: 38" (98cm), 43" (110cm)
47" (122cm)

163

Jacket, skirt, dress, sleeveless jacket and bag

Jacket with casing *model 1*

Pattern pieces: front panel, back panel, casing, front neckline facing, back neckline facing.

Sewing instructions:
1 Reproduce the pattern pieces. With right sides together, fold the fabric in half and pin the pieces to it, having the middle of the back and the middle of the back neckline against the fabric fold. Mark the position of the casing.
2 Cut out all the pieces with an extra ⅜" (1cm) for seam allowance.
3 Zigzag around the edges of the pieces.
4 Stitch the back neckline facing to the neckline. Clip the seam allowance.
5 Stitch the front neckline facings to the front neckline. Clip the seam allowance.
6 Stitch the upper arm seams and stitch the side seams of the neckline facings at the same time. Turn the right side out and top-stitch around the neckline.
7 Turn in and stitch the seam allowance at the bottom edge of the sleeves.
8 Stitch the underarm side seams and clip the curve in the seam allowance.
9 Turn in the seam allowance around the casing and stitch the casing to the jacket.
10 Turn in and stitch the seam allowances on the bottom edge and along the middle of the front.
11 Fold a narrow strip of fabric in half lengthwise, stitch around it and thread it through the casing.

Pants *model 1*

Pattern and sewing instructions: Use model 7, page 136.

Blouse *model 2*

Pattern and sewing instructions: Use model 1, page 160.

Sleeveless jacket and short jacket *model 2 and 6*

Pattern pieces: front panel, back panel.
Notions: bias binding.

Sewing instructions:
1 Reproduce the pattern pieces. With right sides together, fold the fabric in half and pin the pieces to it, having the back panel against the fabric fold.
2 The bottom edge and the sides are cut out with an extra ⅜" (1cm) for seam allowance. The remaining edges without a seam allowance.
3 Zigzag around the pieces.
4 Stitch the shoulder seams.
5 Stitch bias binding around the armholes, front edge and neckline. Leave a piece of binding loose on each side of the neckline to make a tie fastening.
6 Stitch the side seams.
7 Turn in and stitch the seam allowance along the bottom edge.

Skirt *model 2*

Pattern pieces: skirt front, skirt back.

Sewing instructions: See model 7, page 143.

Bag *model 2*

Pattern piece: bag
Notions: bias binding

Sewing instructions:
1 Reproduce the pattern piece. Pin it to a double layer of fabric.
2 Cut out the upper edge with an extra ⅜" (1cm) for seam allowance.
3 Zigzag around the pieces.
4 Turn in and stitch the seam allowance on both upper edges.
5 With wrong sides together stitch bias binding around the outer edge of the two pieces of the bag. Leave 2" (5cm) of binding loose on each side.
6 Make the loose ends of binding into loops and sew them down.

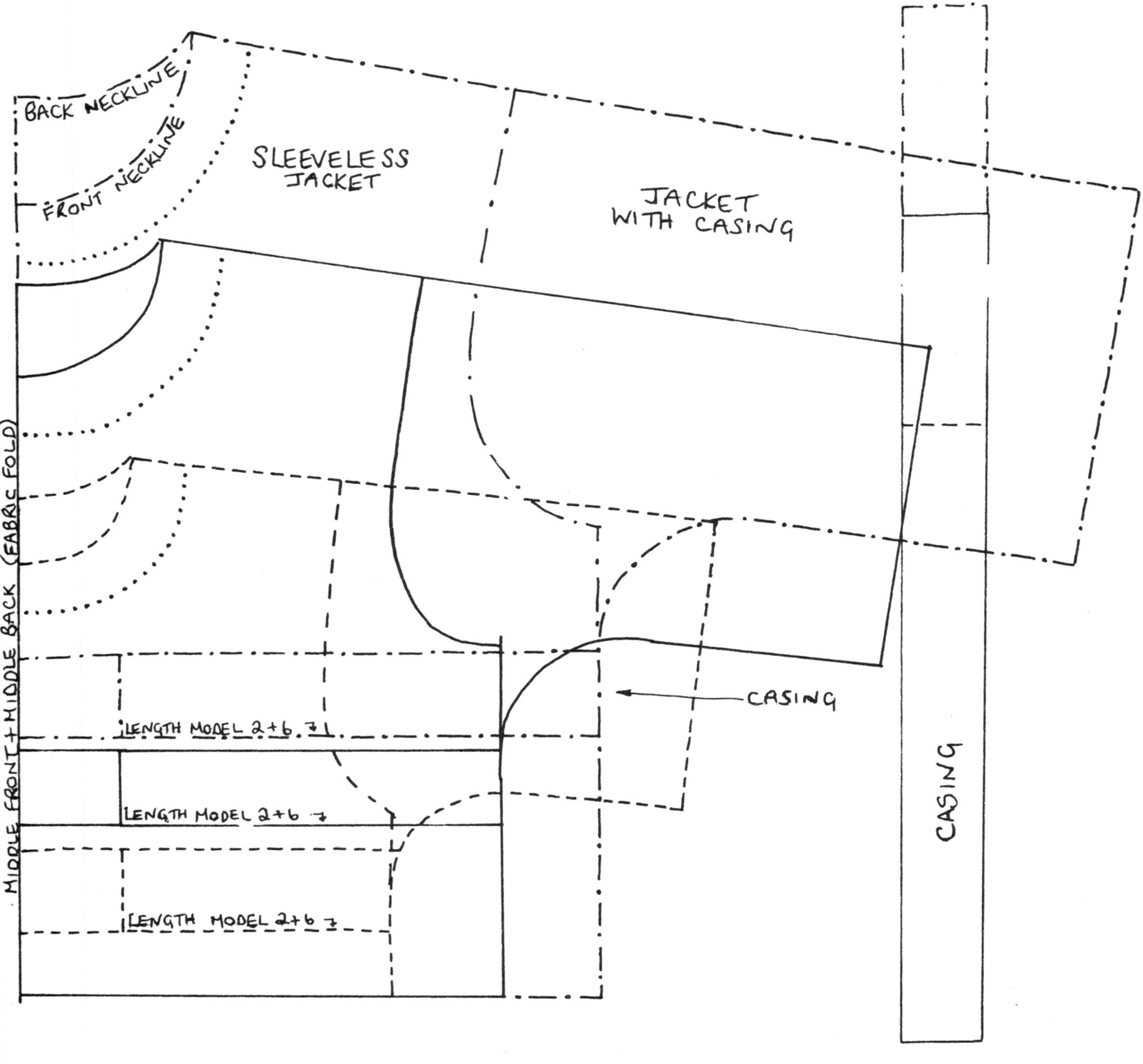

BACK NECKLINE

FRONT NECKLINE

SLEEVELESS
JACKET

JACKET
WITH CASING

MIDDLE FRONT + MIDDLE BACK (FABRIC FOLD)

CASING

CASING

LENGTH MODEL 2+6.7

LENGTH MODEL 2+6.7

LENGTH MODEL 2+6.7

7 Fold a length of bias binding in half lengthwise, stitch it along the edge and then thread it through the loops.
8 To fasten the belt, either tie it or stitch pieces of hook and eye fastening band to the ends.

Pants   model 4

Pattern and sewing instructions: Use model 6, page 136.
The bottom edge of the legs are cut out without a seam allowance, gathered and then stitched around the edge with bias binding. The bias binding should be the same width as the doll's foot.

Dress   model 5

Pattern pieces: front panel, back panel.
Notions: bias binding

Sewing instructions: Use sewing instructions for skirt, page 143.
Fold lengths of bias binding in half lengthwise. Stitch them along the edge to make tapes. Sew the tapes to the top of the skirt to make shoulder bands.

Pants   model 5

Pattern and sewing instructions: Use model 6, page 136.

Knitted sleeveless jacket

First see introduction for instructions about stitches used and size of knitting needles.

Cast on: 24, 32, 38 stitches, according to size.
Knit in plain stitch to 1¾" (4.5cm), 2½" (6.5cm), 3¼" (8.5cm).
Cast off the middle 8, 10, 12 stitches. On one side pick up the shoulder stitches on a reserve strand.
* Continue knitting on one side to a length of 2½" (6.5cm), 3¼" (8.5cm), 4¼" (11cm).
Increase 4, 5, 6 stitches on the neckline side.
Continue knitting to a total length of 4" (10cm), 5½" (14cm), 7" (18cm).
Cast off.
Using the stitches from the reserve strand, repeat in reverse from *.

Construction
Sew a small section of the lower side seams together.

Jacket with collar for your child

Size by age: *3 years,   5 years,   7 years*
Height of child: *38" (98cm), 43" (110cm), 47" (122cm)*

Pattern pieces: front panel, back panel, collar piece, collar piece facing, casing.
Fabric needed: 54" (140cm) wide: 1⅝yd (1.5m)
Notions: 1⅝yd (1.50m) cord, open ended separating zipper.

Sewing instructions:
1 Reproduce the pattern pieces on 2 x 2" (5 x 5cm) dressmaker's pattern paper.
2 With right sides together, fold the fabric in half and pin the pieces to it, having the middle back, the collar, the collar facing and the casing against the fold.

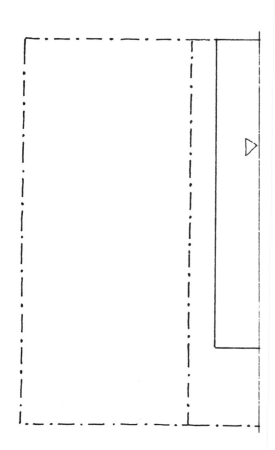

3 The middle of the front is cut out with an extra ¾″ (2cm) for seam allowance. The remaining edges with an extra ⅜-¾″ (1-2cm) for seam allowance.
4 Zigzag around the edges of the pieces.
5 Stitch the upper arm seams.
6 Stitch the underarm side seams. Clip the curve in the seam allowance.
7 Stitch the zipper into the middle of the front (see introduction).
8 Press in the seam allowances around the edges of the casing and stitch on the casing where indicated.
9 Turn in and stitch the seam allowance at the bottom edge of the sleeves.
10 Stitch the collar to the neckline. Clip the seam allowance and press the seam up.

11 With the right sides together stitch the top edge of the collar facing to the top edge of the collar. Clip the curve in the seam allowance. Turn the right side out and press the seam flat. Turn in the bottom edge of the collar. Stitch the collar, keeping close to the neckline.
12 Starting at the stitching on the zipper, top-stitch all the way around the collar.
13 Turn in the bottom edge of the jacket and stitch all the way around.

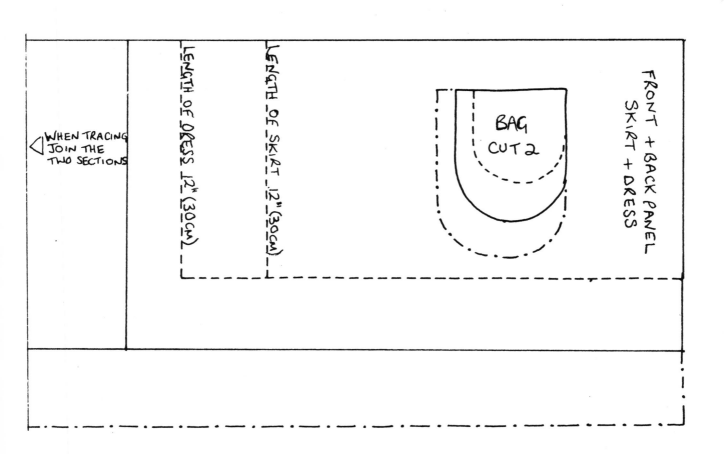

WHEN TRACING JOIN THE TWO SECTIONS

LENGTH OF DRESS 12″ (30CM)

LENGTH OF SKIRT 12″ (30CM)

BAG CUT 2

FRONT + BACK PANEL SKIRT + DRESS

CHILD'S JACKET

CASING

MIDDLE FRONT + BACK

CASING

COLLAR
CUT

Dresses, top, pinafore

Long-sleeved dress   *model 1, 4 and 5*

Pattern pieces: front panel, back panel, yoke, yoke facing, sleeve.
Notions: hook and eye fastening band or buttons and loops, ruched lingerie elastic.

Sewing instructions:
1 Reproduce the pattern pieces. With right sides together, fold the fabric in half and pin the pieces to it, having the middle front of the front panel, yoke and the yoke facing against the fabric fold.
2 Cut out the pieces with an extra ⅜″ (1cm) for seam allowance.
3 Zigzag around the edges of the pieces.
4 Stitch the sleeves to the front and back panel, having the front edge of the sleeve against the raglan side of the front panel. Clip the curve in the seam allowance.
5 Gather the top edge of the front panel, sleeves and back panel until they are the same width as the yoke. Stitch all these to the yoke and clip the seam allowance.
6 Stitch the neckline of the yoke facing to the yoke neckline. Clip the seam allowance.
7 Turn in and stitch the seam allowance on the back sections, stitching the seam allowance on the yoke and the yoke facing at the same time.
8 Turn in the seam allowance at the bottom edge of the sleeves and stitch stretched ruched lingerie elastic to the inside of the bottom edge of the sleeves. Stitch the underarm side seams. Clip the seam allowance.
9 Turn in and stitch the seam allowance on the hemline.
10 Turn in the neckline facing and top-stitch around the neckline.
11 Stitch hook and eye fastening band to the back yoke or sew on buttons and loops.

Top

Pattern pieces: front panel, back panel, front neckline facing, back neckline facing.
Notions: bias binding, hook and eye fastening band.

Sewing instructions:
1 Reproduce the pattern pieces. With right sides together, fold the fabric in half and pin the pieces to it, having the middle front against the fabric fold.
2 Cut out the pieces with an extra ⅜″ (1cm) for seam allowance. The bottom edge and the side edge are cut out without a seam allowance.
3 Zigzag around the edges of the pieces.
4 Stitch the front facing to the neckline. Clip the seam allowance.
5 Stitch the back neckline facings to the neckline. Clip the seam allowance.
6 Stitch the shoulder seams, stitching the facing shoulder seams at the same time.
7 Turn in the facing and top-stitch around the neckline.
8 Stitch bias binding around the side edges.
9 Stitch bias binding along the bottom edge of the front panel. Leave a piece of binding loose on each side to make a tie fastening.
10 Stitch bias binding along the bottom edges of the back panels. Leave a piece of binding loose on each outer end to make a tie fastening.
11 Turn in the seam allowance on the middle of the back and stitch. Then sew on hook and eye fastening band.

Dress   *model 2*

Pattern pieces: front panel, back panel, yoke, yoke facing, sleeve.
Notions: strip of lace, ruched lingerie elastic ⅜″ (1cm) wide, hook and eye fastening band or buttons and loops.

Sewing instructions:
Follow the instructions for model 1. The only difference is in step 5.
5 Gather a strip of lace at the same time as you gather the top edge. The strip of lace must be the same length as the fabric which is to be gathered.
Stitch strips of lace to the dress and the sleeves.

Short-sleeved dress *model 2*

Pattern pieces: front panel, back panel, sleeve, yoke, yoke facing.

Notions: hook and eye fastening band or buttons and loops, ruched lingerie elastic.

Sewing instructions:
Follow the instructions for model 1.

Coat *model 5*

Pattern pieces: front panel, back panel, yoke, hood.

Sewing instructions:
1 Reproduce the pattern pieces. With right sides together, fold the fabric in half and pin the pieces to it having the middle of the back against the fabric fold.
2 Cut out the pieces with an extra ⅜" (1cm) for seam allowance. Cut out the hood once again in lining fabric.
3 Zigzag around the edges of the pieces.
4 Stitch the sleeves to the front and back panel, having the front side of the sleeve against the raglan edge of the front panel. Clip the curve in the seam allowance.
5 Gather the top edge of the front panel, sleeves and back panel until they are the same width as the yoke. Stitch everything to the yoke. Clip the seam allowance of the yoke.
6 Stitch the hood sections together. Clip the seam allowance.
7 Stitch the lining sections of the hood together. Clip the seam allowance.
8 Turn in and stitch the edges of the middle front. On the yoke section stitch on narrow tapes made out of bias binding. Fold the binding in half lengthwise and stitch along the edges. Stitch the tapes on at the same time as you stitch the middle front edges.
9 Stitch the hood to the neckline. Clip the seam allowance.
10 Stitch the front edges of the hoods together. Clip the seam allowance of the lining hood. Turn this in and sew the bottom edge to the neckline.
11 Turn in and stitch the seam allowance at the bottom of the sleeves.
12 Stitch the underarm side seams. Clip the curve in the seam allowance.
13 Turn in and stitch the hemline.

Pinafore *model 6*

Pattern pieces: front panel, back panel, yoke, yoke facing, frill.

Notions: hook and eye fastening band or buttons and loops.

Sewing instructions:
1 Reproduce the pattern pieces. With right sides together, fold the fabric in half and pin the pieces to it, having the middle front of the yoke and middle front of the yoke facing against the fabric fold. Mark the yoke to show where the front and the back panel will be attached.
2 Cut out the pieces with an extra ⅜" (1cm) for seam allowance. Cut out the yoke facing ⅜" (1cm) shorter on the bottom edge.
3 Zigzag around the edges.
4 Turn in and stitch the seam allowance on one side of the frill.
5 Turn in and stitch the seam allowance around the armholes.
6 Gather the frill until it is the same width as the yoke. Stitch it around the yoke.
7 Gather the front panel and the back panel until they are the width indicated on the yoke. Stitch them to the yoke. Clip the seam allowance of the yoke. Press the seam allowance up and stitch all the way around the edge on the right side.
8 Stitch the side seams.
9 Stitch the yoke facing to the neckline. Clip the seam allowance. Turn the right side out and top-stitch all the way around the neckline.
10 Turn in and stitch the seam allowance along the middle of the back.

175

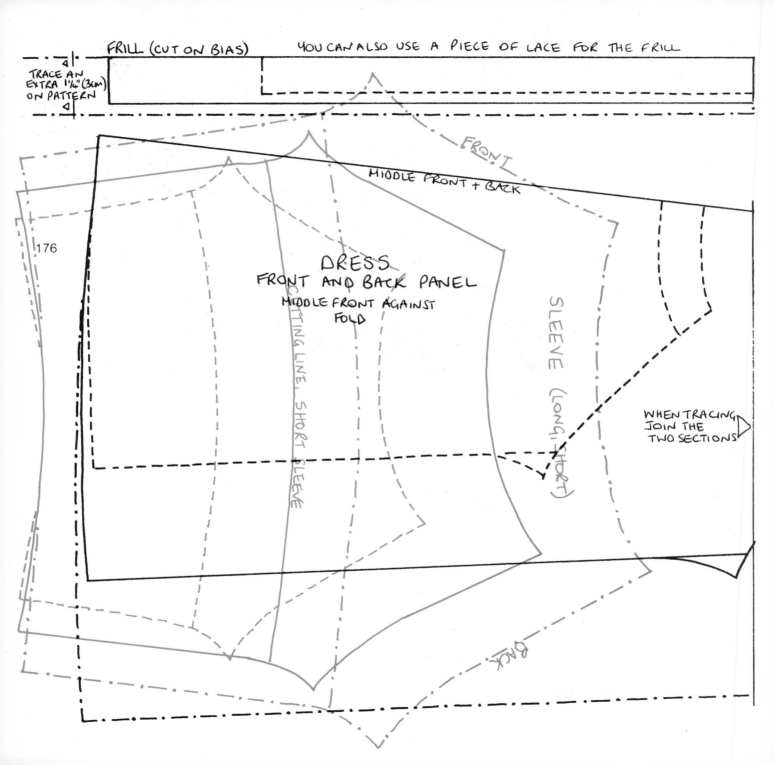

FRILL (CUT ON BIAS)   YOU CAN ALSO USE A PIECE OF LACE FOR THE FRILL

TRACE AN
EXTRA 1¼" (3cm)
ON PATTERN

MIDDLE FRONT + BACK

FRONT

176

DRESS
FRONT AND BACK PANEL
MIDDLE FRONT AGAINST
FOLD

CUTTING LINE, SHORT SLEEVE

SLEEVE (LONG, SHORT)

WHEN TRACING
JOIN THE
TWO SECTIONS

BACK

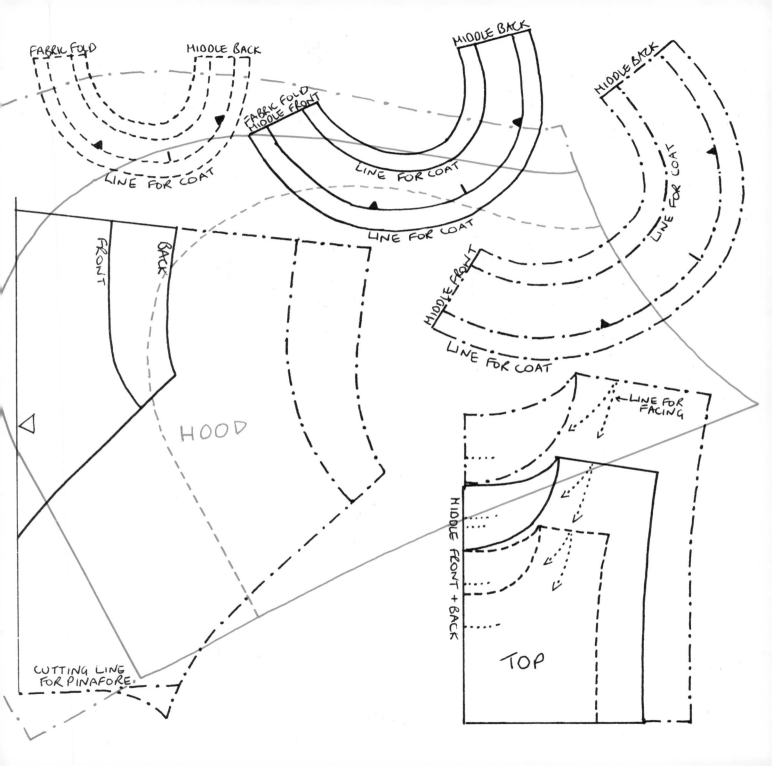

Child's dress with top

Size by age: *3 years,   5 years,   7 years*
Height of child: *38" (98cm), 43" (110cm), 47" (122cm)*

Pattern pieces: front panel, back panel, yoke, yoke facing, sleeve.
Fabric needed: 36" (90cm) wide: 3¾yd (3.5m)
54" (140cm) wide: 2yd (1.85m)
Notions: zipper, elastic.

Sewing instructions:

1 Reproduce the pattern pieces. Mark the sleeve to indicate which is the front and which is the back.
2 With right sides together, fold the fabric in half and pin the pieces to it, having the middle front of the front panel and the yoke against the fabric fold.
3 Cut out the bottom edge of the sleeves with an extra 1" (2.5cm) for seam allowance. The remaining edges with an extra ⅜-¾" (1-2cm) for seam allowance.
4 Zigzag around the edges of the pieces.
5 Stitch the sleeves to the front and back panel, having the front of the sleeve against the raglan edge of the front panel. Clip the curve in the seam allowance and press the seams open.
6 Gather the top edge of the front panel, the sleeves and the back panel until they are the same width as the yoke. Stitch them all to the yoke. Clip the seam allowance of the yoke. Press the seam allowance up.
7 Stitch the neckline of the yoke facing to the yoke neckline. Clip the seam allowance.
8 Stitch the middle back seam. Press this open.
9 Stitch the zipper into the middle back seam (see introduction).
10 Turn in the neckline facing, turn in the seam allowance on the middle back of the facing and stitch all the way around the neckline.
11 Baste the facing to lie flat against the yoke and topstitch on the right side all the way around the bottom edge of the yoke.
12 Stitch the underarm side seams. Clip the curve in the seam allowance and press the seam open.
13 Turn in the seam allowance at the bottom edge of the sleeve and stitch ¾" (2cm) from the bottom edge. Leave a small opening for the elastic.
14 Turn in and stitch the hemline.
15 Thread elastic through the casings and stitch the ends.

Top

Pattern pieces: front panel, back panel.
Fabric needed: 36" (90cm) wide: ⅝yd (0.3m)
54" (140cm) wide: ⅝yd (0.3m)
Notions: 3¾yd (3.5m) bias binding, button.

Sewing instructions:

1 Reproduce the pattern pieces on 2 x 2" (5 x 5cm) dressmaker's pattern paper.
2 With right sides together, fold the fabric in half and pin the pieces to it, having the middle front against the fabric fold.
3 Cut out the bottom edge, the side edge and the neckline without a seam allowance. The remaining edges with an extra ⅜-¾" (1-2cm) for seam allowance.
4 Zigzag around the pieces.
5 Stitch the shoulder seams and press them open.
6 Stitch bias binding around the side edges.
7 Stitch the seam down the middle of the back, leaving a small opening at the top.
8 Stitch bias binding around the bottom edge of the front panel. Leave 12" (30cm) of binding loose on each side to make a tie fastening.
9 Stitch bias binding along the bottom edge of the back panel. Leave 12" (30cm) of binding loose on each side to make a tie fastening.
10 Stitch bias binding around the neckline. Leave 2¼" (6cm) loose on one side for a loop.
11 Stitch along the edges of the opening. At the same time stitch down the end of the loop.
12 Sew a button at the top of the opening.

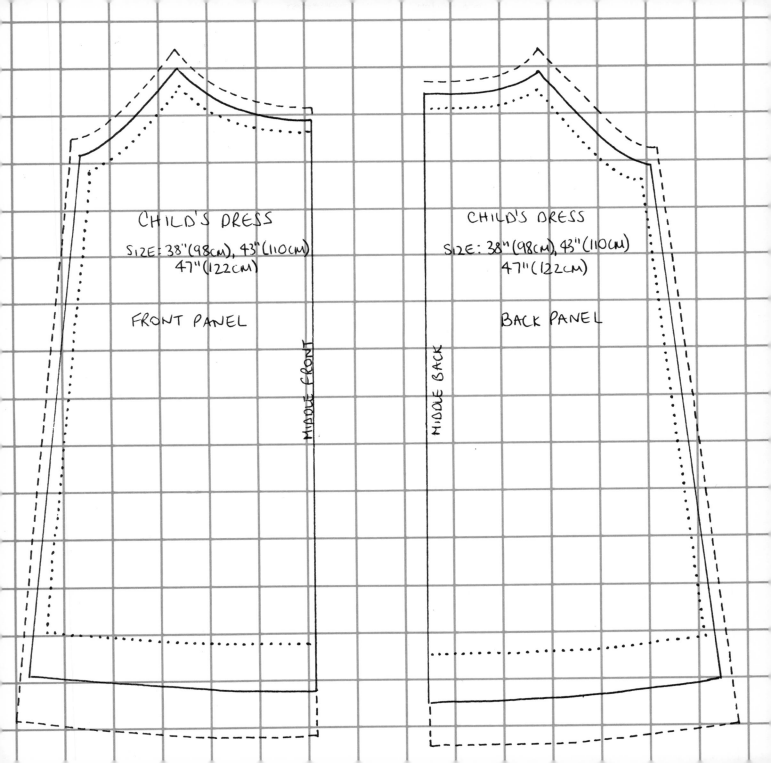

CHILD'S DRESS

SIZE: 38"(98CM), 43"(110CM) 47"(122CM)

FRONT PANEL

MIDDLE FRONT

CHILD'S DRESS

SIZE: 38"(98CM), 43"(110CM) 47"(122CM)

BACK PANEL

MIDDLE BACK

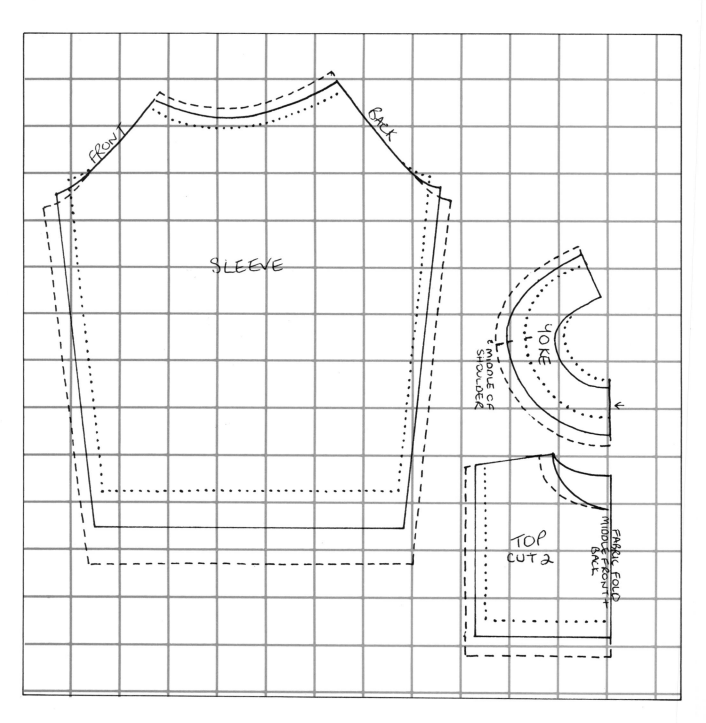

180

SLEEVE

FRONT

BACK

YOKE

MIDDLE C.F.
SHOULDER

TOP
CUT 2

MIDDLE FRONT +
MIDDLE BACK

FABRIC FOLD

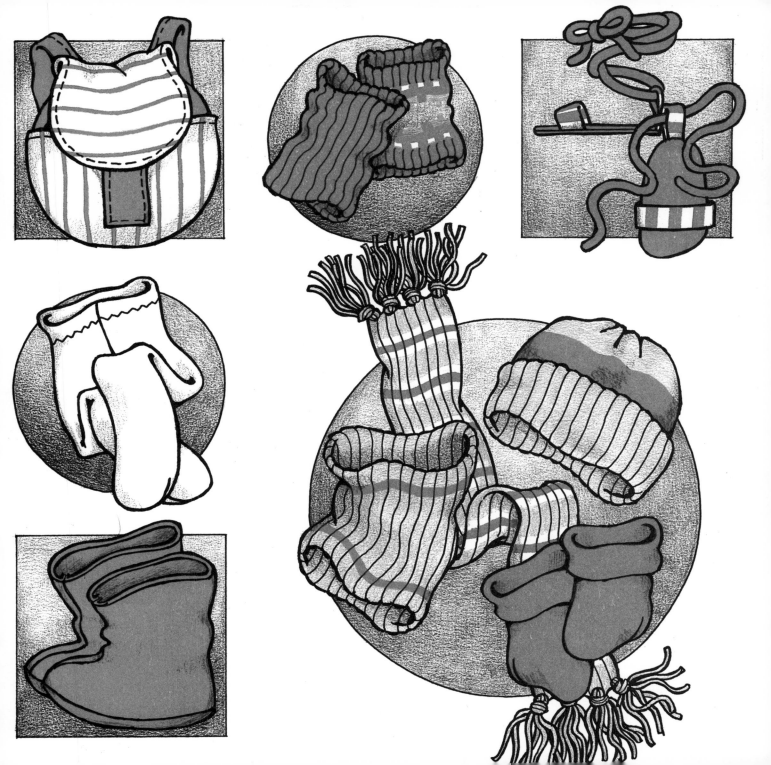

Backpack, footwear, pantyhose, scarf and hat

Doll's backpack

Pattern pieces: front panel, back panel, flap, pocket, tab, strap.

Notions: small rings, cord, hook and eye fastening band or 1 snap fastener.

Sewing instructions:

1 Reproduce the pattern pieces. Fold the fabric in half and pin the pieces to it against the fabric fold. Mark the position of the pocket and the flap.
2 Cut out the pattern pieces with an extra ⅜" (1cm) for seam allowance. Cut out the flap twice.
3 Zigzag around the pieces.
4 Fold the tab in half and stitch around it, leaving one edge open. Clip the corners. Turn the right side out and stitch around the edges. At the same time stitch a piece of hook and eye fastening band to the underside of the tab.
5 Stitch the flap sections together. At the same time stitch on the top edge of the tab. Clip the seam allowance and turn the right side out. Top-stitch all the way around the edge.
6 Turn in the seam allowance along the top edge of the flap and stitch the flap where indicated on the back panel.
7 Turn in and stitch the seam allowance along the top edge of the front and the back panel.
8 Turn in and stitch the seam allowance on the top edge of the pocket. Stitch a piece of hook and eye fastening band on to the pocket. Pin the pockert where indicated on the front panel.
9 Fold the straps in half lengthwise and stitch them along the edge.
10 Stitch the front and the back section together. At the same time stitch on the straps where indicated. Clip the seam allowance and turn the right side out.
11 Sew rings to the top edge of the front and the back sections and thread a cord through them.
12 Sew the top edge of the straps to the flap where indicated.
Stitch the top edge.

Sandals

Pattern pieces: sole, heel strap, instep band.
Notions: cord, strip of leather, glue.

Instructions:

1 Reproduce the pattern pieces. Place them on soft leather or imitation leather.
2 Cut out the instep band with an extra ⅜" (1cm) for seam allowance on the sides. The heel strap has a seam allowance of ¾" (2cm) along the top edge. The sole, the sides of the heel strap and the top and bottom edge of the instep band are all cut out without a seam allowance. Cut out the sole twice.
3 Fold the heel strap in half.
4 Glue the two soles together. Glue the seam allowance of the heel strap and the seam allowances of the instep band where indicated between the two soles. The heel strap now forms a loop.
5 Thread a cord or strip of leather through the loop.

To make the second sandal, turn the pattern piece for the sole to face in the opposite direction. Cut it out and repeat steps 2-5.

Boots

Pattern pieces: sole, boot.

Sewing instructions:

1 Trace the pattern pieces. Place them on a double layer of imitation leather, soft leather, felt or plastic.
2 Cut out the top edge without a seam allowance. The remaining edges with an extra ¼" (0.5cm) for seam allowance. Cut out the boot twice.
3 If you wish zigzag around the pieces.
4 Stitch the front and the back together. Clip the seam allowance.
5 Stitch the sole onto the foot. Clip the seam allowance and turn the right side out.

Pantyhose

Pattern pieces: front panel, back panel
Notions: elastic

Sewing instructions:
1 Reproduce the pattern. Mark the highest side and the lowest side. Place the pattern pieces on a double layer of fabric (use an old pair of wool pantyhose or a thin pullover). Pin both pieces against the fabric fold. Mark the point up to which the seam is to be stitched.
2 The front of the pantyhose is cut lower than the back. Cut out the top edge with an extra ⅜″ (1cm) for seam allowance. The remaining edges with an extra ¼″ (0.5cm) for seam allowance.
3 Stitch the inside leg seams by hand or using a zigzag stitch as far as the mark. Zigzag both edges of the seam allowance together.
4 Stitch the crotch seam with a zigzag stitch or by hand. Zigzag both edges of the seam allowance.
5 Turn in the seam allowance along the top edge and zigzag or sew this down by hand. Leave a small opening in the middle of the back for the elastic.
6 Thread elastic through the casing and sew the ends together.

Socks

Sewing instructions:
1 Reproduce the pattern pieces. With right sides together, fold the fabric in half and pin the pieces to it, having the side against the fabric fold. Mark the point up to which the seam is to be stitched.
2 Cut out with an extra ¼″ (0.5cm) for seam allowance.
3 Turn in and stitch the seam allowance along the top edge.
4 Stitch the inside leg seam as far as the mark. Zigzag both edges of the seam allowance together.

Knitting: first see introduction for instructions about stitches used and size of knitting needles.

Leg warmers

Cast on: 16, 22, 28 stitches, according to size.
Knit in rib stitch to 1½″ (4cm), 2¼″ (6cm), 3¼″ (8cm).
Cast off and sew up the seam.

Legwarmers in jacquard pattern

Cast on: 16, 22, 28 stitches, according to size.
Knit in rib stitch for ⅜″ (1cm).
Continue in stocking stitch.
Knit in jacquard pattern to a length of 1¼″ (3cm), 2″ (5cm), 2¾″ (7cm).
Continue knitting in rib stitch to a length of 1½″ (4cm), 2¼″ (6cm), 3¼″ (8cm).
Cast off and sew up the seam.

Scarf

Cast on: 4, 6, 8 stitches, according to size.
Knit in rib stitch to a length of 11″ (28cm), 14″ (36cm), 17¼″ (44cm).
Cast off.
Optional: make a fringe at both ends.

Hat

Cast on: 36, 48, 60 stitches, according to size.
Knit in rib stitch to a length of 1½″ (4cm), 2¼″ (5.5cm), 2¾″ (7cm).
Continue in stocking stitch. Knit to 3½″ (9cm), 4½″ (11.5cm), 5½″ (14cm).
For the next two rows knit two stitches together.
Cast off the remaining stitches.
Sew up the seam and then thread a strand of wool through the top stitches of the hat. Pull the thread tight and stitch it down.

Neckwarmer

Cast on: 36, 46, 56 stitches, according to size.
Knit in rib stitch to a length of 1½″ (4cm), 2¼″ (5.5cm), 2¾″ (7cm).
Cast off.
Sew up the seam.

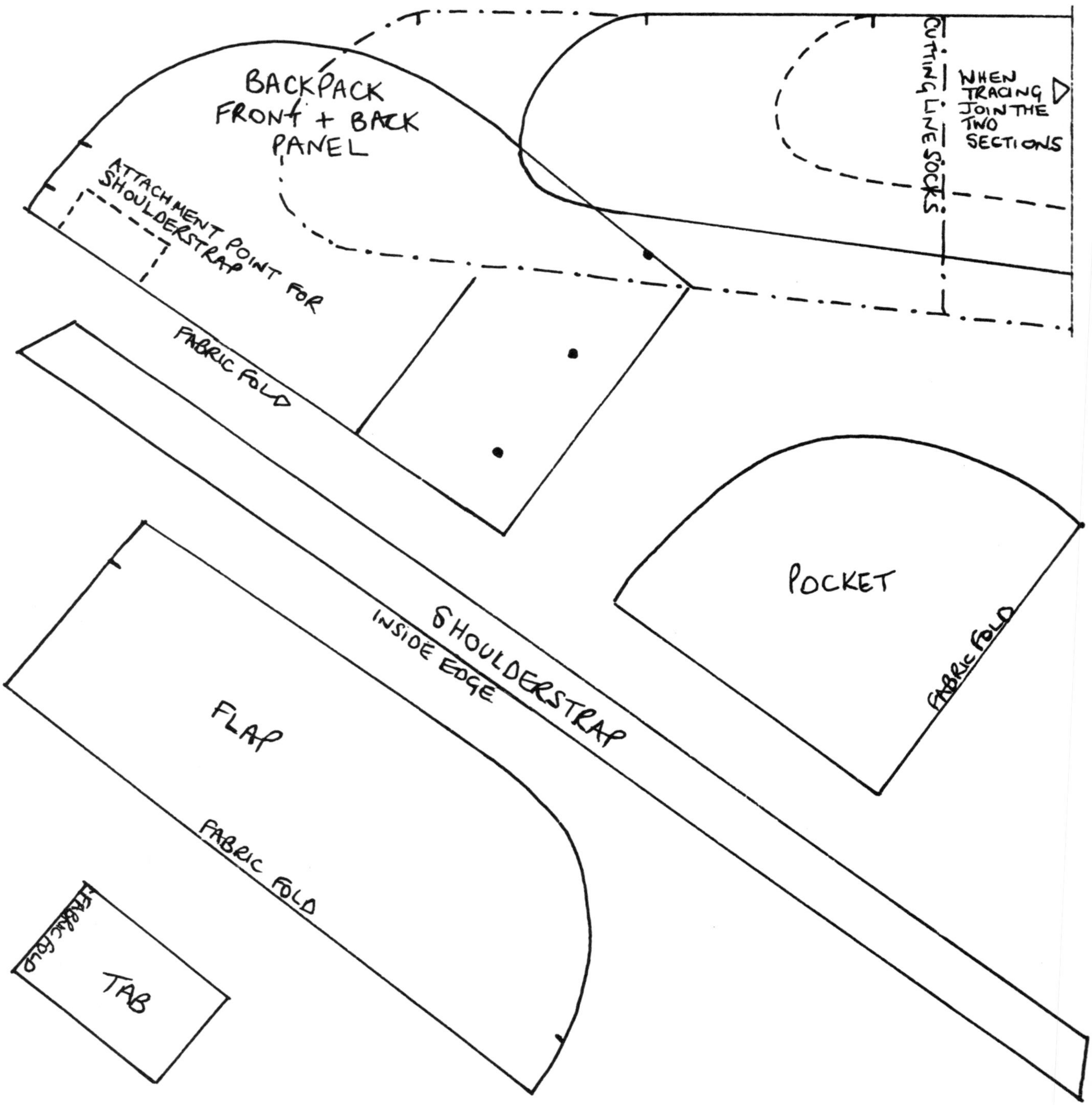

BACKPACK
FRONT + BACK
PANEL

ATTACHMENT POINT FOR
SHOULDERSTRAP

CUTTING LINE SOCKS

WHEN
TRACING
JOIN THE
TWO
SECTIONS

184

FABRIC FOLD

POCKET

FABRIC FOLD

SHOULDERSTRAP
INSIDE EDGE

FLAP

FABRIC FOLD

FABRIC FOLD

TAB

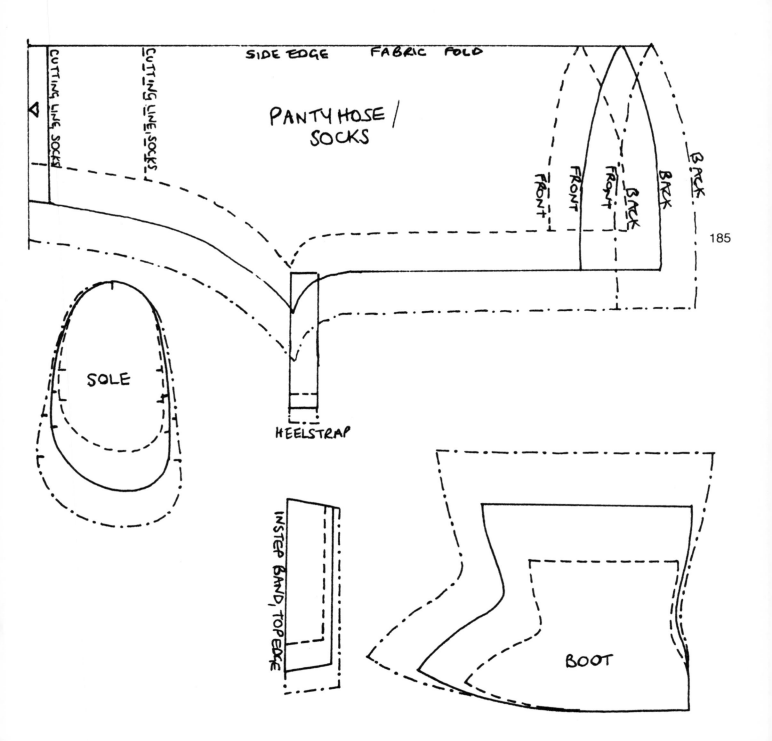

PANTY HOSE /
SOCKS

SIDE EDGE   FABRIC FOLD

CUTTING LINE, SOCKS

CUTTING LINE, SOCKS

FRONT

FRONT

BACK FRONT

BACK

BACK

185

SOLE

HEELSTRAP

INSTEP BAND, TOP EDGE

BOOT

Other interesting books from Exley Publications:

Little Clothes for Little People, £10.95 (hb)
In the same series, this book contains 133 original designs to make a complete wardrobe of clothes for babies, toddlers and children up to the age of 7 – from bibs to playsuits, overalls to ponchos, trousers to party dresses. With a scale pattern for each design and step-by-step instructions, this book makes a practical, imaginative present.

Look, Listen and Play, £7.95 (hb)
This unusual activity book for 3 to 6 year olds combines a children's story with dozens of activities to help children learn such concepts as counting, near and far, high and low, big and small, loud and soft. With whimsical drawings throughout, this book will provide endless fascination for small children.

Father Gander's Nursery Rhymes, £6.95 (hb)
This collection of non-sexist, traditional nursery rhymes will help little girls and boys to grow up feeling truly equal. Without losing the charm and melody of the originals, this collection offers parents and teachers an alternative that could have a positive impact on the personalities and perceptions of a whole generation of young children.

Minou, £5.95 (hb)
This is a beautifully-illustrated story about Minou, a Siamese cat living in Paris. When her mistress is taken away in an ambulance, Minou finds herself with no one to look after her. She has to learn to stand on her own feet – to feed and look after herself. By identifying with Minou, this book will help young children – especially little girls – to think and act independently.

It Worked for Me, £5.95 (hb)
Over 1,000 practical tips for coping with young children, including dealing with tantrums, crying and sleeplessness, child-proofing the home, medical and other emergencies as well as ways to encourage self-esteem in children. A useful book for all parents with young children.

Feeding Your Child, £8.95 (hb)
Sound, practical advice on the correct feeding of babies and young children. We now know that wrong eating habits in the first few years of life can carry right through to adult life: an early sweet tooth leads to dental caries and, maybe, diabetes, overfed babies tend to become fatties as adults, too much fat can lead to heart problems, cancer and multiple sclerosis. The author is a nutritionist and a mother, and her book will be of great value to other young parents.

Help! I've Got a Kid!, £6.95 (hb)
An extremely practical handbook for parents suffering their children's tantrums, screaming, fights and so on. Parents often do not realise that it is their efforts to cope with such behaviour that is encouraging the child to continue with it. Illustrated throughout with strip cartoons, the book provides a step-by-step guide for improving undesirable behaviour.

How To Win at Housework, £7.95 (hb)
When you run a house, things go wrong. The drains block, spills ruin carpets, coffee mug rings ruin furniture. This book gives the answers to the 100 most common problems in running a home.

Who Says It's A Woman's Job To Clean?, £7.95 (hb)
Men say they do their fair share of work around the house, but according to the author of this book, they kid themselves. The book highlights what they do – and don't do, demolishes the familiar male excuses and comes up with a plan for action. A fun gift and essential reading for all men!

The Secret of Freedom From Clutter, £7.95 (hb), £4.95 (pb)
This book sets out to show how damaging junk is in people's lives. Junk has to be tidied, stored and insured and time spent dealing with junk is time lost for more important things. Through anecdotes, charts and quizzes, the book offers practical advice on how to deal with clutter. For all who have waged war on clutter and lost, here is the inspiration to get the job done once and for all!

Free colour catalogue available on request. Books may be ordered through your bookshop or by post from Exley Publications, 16 Chalk Hill, Watford, Herts, United Kingdom, WD1 4BN. Please add £1 per book for postage and packing. Maximum postage £2.